RESCUED

FROM DRUGS TO JESUS

BY

COURTNEY SMITH

Table of Contents

———— ✳ ————

This book is dedicated to my amazing parents who loved me through my lost ways. You knew God had a plan for me and you fervently prayed. Thank you for laying me at God's feet so that I may live out my brokenness for God to use to His glory.

Prologue

Pure Darkness

———— ❋ ————

"Turn away from me so I can have a moment's joy before I go to the place of no return, to the land of gloom and utter darkness, to the land of deepest night, of utter darkness and disorder, where even the light is like darkness." -Job 10:20-22

I never thought in a million years that I would be here in this place. A place dark and cold. As I slowly walk through this house, it is like watching a scene from a movie. There are half-burned candles lighting the way. The wax drips down the side of the candles and onto the worn furniture. There doesn't appear to be any electricity. The house is full of people sprawled out over the couches and floors, some seemingly in their own thoughtful bliss, and others fidgeting and preoccupied with who knows what. Many appear to be wasting away with a dull, dead look in their eyes. It is dirty and unkempt. I'm standing in the middle of a crack house, taking in the surroundings and I know deep down, I am not supposed to be here.

I am so scared, I am trembling inside, but I can't show the sheer panic I feel, or I may put myself in danger. There are about twenty people around me and straight in front of me is my friend, smoking crack with a random dealer. I had been around drugs before and had even used drugs, but never had I been around crack, let alone in a real crack house. My reality did not fully comprehend there could even be places like this. Why would anyone want to live this way? This is something only on TV or in the movies, right?

All I want to do is run, run away as fast as I can, but I stand frozen, paralyzed. Why can't I take control of my body and move? I have no idea who these people are, and I don't know how they are going to react if I do decide to leave, and even then—do I want to leave my friends and walk away by myself in the middle of the night? Not only do I not know where we are, but also I know we are not in a safe neighborhood. A thousand questions; a thousand thoughts ran through my mind.

I decided to stay because I was with two of my guy friends, my big guy friends. They would protect me if anything went wrong. My boyfriend and I were not even supposed to go into the house. We were to wait for our friend out in the car, who was to be only five minutes. After forty-five minutes of waiting, we decided to go in and make sure everything was okay. I did not want to go in, but I did not want to stay in the car by myself either.

As it turned out, our friend was okay, but the drug dealer, to my dismay, decided to invite us to have a seat and join him. I reluctantly sat on the dirt-stained couch in hopes we would leave before anything happens I could not take back. The dealer turned his attention to me, a young nineteen-year-old pretty girl unlike any of the other women who normally hang out in a place like this. My heart began to pound out of my chest and I grabbed my boyfriend's hand and squeezed it.

He appeared nice and he asked me if I would like a hit. I told him, "No thank you." I wanted to tell him that I did drugs, but not crack. Never crack. Instead, I sat still. He must have sensed I have never tried it and asked me, more as a statement than a question, "You have never smoked crack before, have you?"

"No, I have not," I said, trying to sound like it was no big deal.

Without missing a beat, he explained it is the best feeling in the world and insisted I try it. "You should try it; here, I'll show you."

My mind raced, what was I to do? He was quite scary to me, and crack was not something I wanted to get into, but even though I was scared, even with the nagging feeling that I shouldn't, I tried crack for the first time. Not only did I try it, but I did it all night long until there was no more left to smoke and no more money to spend for the night.

Chapter 1

My Childhood

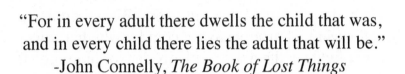

"For in every adult there dwells the child that was, and in every child there lies the adult that will be."
-John Connelly, *The Book of Lost Things*

$\mathscr{G}$rowing up in my home was like going on several different roller coasters. Some of our adventures were exciting— full of speed, loops, screams, and laughter. Other times it was like that old wooden roller coaster—bumpy the whole way through, but no matter the situation with my family, we got through it together. When I was about twelve, we went on a cross country road trip from California to Ohio and my father, in response to anything that would happen, especially negative stuff, would always say, "Remember kids, it is all part of the adventure." It was his way of helping us to stay positive no matter what happened. To this day, we still quote him through the good times and the bad.

I grew up in a Christian home and am the oldest of four children – two boys and two girls. Let's say our house was rarely quiet. We lived on the end of a cul-de-sac with lots of kids our age. Kids always came in and out of our house. We spent many nights with the neighborhood kids playing games outside with not a care in the world until mom would yell out the front door "Dinner time!" Honestly, there couldn't have been a better neighborhood in which to grow up. I will forever remember the two-story house in Tracy during my adolescent years. We would try to get in as much trouble as we could—whether it was water fights in the house with my dad, or jumping off our roof onto our big trampoline and then into our pool (when our parents weren't home). We would even play hide and go seek in the house with my dad, where his favorite place to hide was the laundry chute between the second and first floors. It amazes me there were not more trips to the emergency room.

My parents loved to spend family time. It was much easier to get us all together when we were younger, but I remember TGIF where we would make pizza, popcorn, and soda and watch all of the family shows that were on every Friday night. These were the days when "Full House", "Family Matters", and other family-oriented shows were on. It was the only night we were allowed to stay up until ten each week. We would have game and movie nights, and for the most part we would watch football together on Sundays. Go 49ers! One of my fondest memories is when my dad spent several nights reading *Narnia* to all of us kids. We would race upstairs and jump on his bed and he would read a chapter to us every night. I didn't think much of it then, but looking back on it now, my parents made sure we had special unique moments to remember. Not only did we have family time, but my parents would spend individual time with each of as well. Making sure each of us kids knew our parents loved us. My dad would spend time with me practicing basketball, and my mom and I would spend special days shopping and sharing our love for shoes. My parents weren't perfect, but they came pretty close, always making sure we knew we were loved.

"Follow God's example, therefore, as dearly loved children and walk in the way of love, just as Christ loved us and gave himself up for us as a fragrant offering and sacrifice to God." —Ephesians 5:1-2

It was important to my parents to teach us the morals and values of their Christian faith. We went to church every Sunday and as a family we were heavily involved. I remember my dad would usher, and my mom would play piano. All of us kids would be in the children's plays during the holidays and were involved in all of the youth groups. Church was a fun place to go. All of our friends were there and it was a constructive place for us to be.

When you grow up in the church, your whole life, your spiritual beliefs tend to be your parents' beliefs until you accept them as your own. I believe there is a moment in your life where an individual makes the choice to have a personal relationship with Christ. Some people make that choice from early on and live their faith throughout the full cycle of their life, maturing as they get older. Some people may push away from the faith and church all together, never adopting it. Or you could be like me, wavering back and forth in uncertainty until adulthood.

I loved going to church, but it was primarily because of the people that were there and the relationships I had with my friends. I went to church because we went as a family and it was fun, but not because I wanted to learn more about God. There were times in which I was more apt to study God's Word and that was when I was interested in or dating someone. As I started my senior year in high school I started to push away from the church and my faith. The pleasures of this world were a lot more enticing and I wanted to explore beyond the realms of the boundaries within which I was raised. What was it in my personality that caused me to drift away? I knew there was a God and I knew all of the different stories of the Bible, but for some reason, my heart didn't connect to the knowledge I had obtained throughout the years.

My mom once told me that I loved attention growing up. I would intentionally seek it out anywhere I went. Here is what my mom said, in her own words:

When Courtney was about three years old, we were walking in the mall. We began to pass an electronics store that was advertising televisions in the window and there was an aerobics or dance program being played. This caught Courtney's attention and she stopped and started mimicking what was on the television. I have to admit, it was the cutest thing. People stopped and made comments on how cute she was and it was clear that, even at that tender age, she recognized the attention and doubled her efforts, all the while grinning from ear to ear.

Sadly, in the long run, that type of attention, for my personality, turned into a stronger desire for me to be selfish. It was all about me—what I wanted to do, my looks, my clothes. I was definitely into myself growing up. Honestly, I don't know how much of that is normal for a teenage girl and how much is not. However, I do remember my family— mainly my brothers and sister—would make fun of me because every time I walked by a mirror, any mirror, I would look at myself to make sure my hair was in place and I looked up to the standards I had made for myself. On a side note, if only I knew all of the style tricks I know now. I look back at some of my style choices back then and I ask myself, *what was I thinking?* But I digress.

Due to my selfish nature, I was manipulative, especially in my teen years. I would actually weigh my possible punishments against the things I wanted to do that my parents had prohibited. Was sneaking out of the house to go to a party worth two weeks' grounding? If the punishment was worth it, I would do it, if it wasn't, I wouldn't do it. In my dad's own words:

> Courtney was quite the master when it came to defying the rules. It wasn't that she was trying to be clever and hide what she was doing or even come up with some conceived "misunderstanding" of what the rules were. No, for her, it was quite simple. If she wanted to do the forbidden acts badly enough, she would suck it up and just take the punishment. I remember one time telling her that she could not ride her bike past a certain point in the neighborhood. The punishment was a spanking with the famous "board of education" that I had made. She carefully considered the consequence and decided that the pleasure and freedom of going beyond the boundary was worth the pain of the spanking. Needless to say, it required some creative parenting on our part to find consequences that were effective for her.

As he said, it forced them to get creative with some of my punishments. Let's say I spent a lot of time in my room without any television, and boy, did I love my shows.

On the outside, I projected strong confidence, but on the inside, I was insecure. Where did that insecurity come from? Honestly, I don't know. It was probably a combination of things, but the only thing I could think of were kids bullying me when I was little. I know I am not the only one who suffered in this way, but when it is happening, it feels that way. It amazes me how cruel kids can be and how it was torture going through the cruelty of the verbal attacks. But yet somehow I still wanted to be part of that same group. Everyone wants to belong to something and to feel accepted. The kids would chase me and make pig noises, grunting and calling me a pig because my nose is a little turned up. Or in junior high when I had bad acne, they would ask me how I could have chicken pox again when I had them last week.

Whatever confidence I had as a little girl dancing in the malls was washed away every time I went to school. Each time I did anything going forward, I would analyze the situation over and over again, worried that my actions would look stupid. I had this constant fear of how people would think of me and having that lifelong need for attention and acceptance, I tried to please everyone around me. With this thought process, I turned into what people wanted me to be instead of becoming my own person. Whatever group I was with would dictate I how I changed my personality. I could never get a handle on it and so personality fluctuations and attention-seeking behavior followed me into my early adulthood.

In junior high and high school, I found a constructive outlet for this attention-seeking behavior through sports. I played basketball in junior high and high school along with volleyball. Playing in games where I could highlight myself alongside a team atmosphere was the perfect setting to complement my desires to be in the limelight. In my senior year in high school I had the nickname Courtney "From Downtown" Smith. Three pointers were my specialty. There was one game where I hit five three-pointers in the first half of the basketball game. I was on fire. I had no idea how I made so many, but they kept going *swish, swish, swish.* The crowd stood and screamed every time I made a basketball. If there were one moment in my life I would like to do over and over again, it would be this moment. All eyes were on what I would do next and I absolutely loved it. The team walked into the locker room during half time and my coach said not to sit down because I would cool off. I was flaming hot. That game I scored eighteen points, the best game of my life. Every newspaper interviewed me after the game. My parents couldn't stop talking about it. I ended up awarded athlete of the week for the county newspaper, athlete of the month from the city, and a few other awards that year.

I write this event in detail because it is important to know the feelings I lived for, the emotion I constantly longed for, the trigger that would put me over the top. I thrived that night especially feeling like I was accepted and loved by my peers. That is what I had always wanted from the time I danced in the malls through my teenage years: love and acceptance. I felt I had finally achieved it from my peers. The adrenaline that ran through my veins was an unbelievable feeling. A feeling that would become an addiction, an unhealthy addiction. I became addicted to acceptance and stature.

I read a psychology article that said:

Peer acceptance is measured by the quality rather than the quantity of a child or adolescent's relationships. While the number of friends varies among children and over time as a child develops, peer acceptance is often established as early as preschool. Factors such as physical attractiveness, cultural traits, and disabilities affect the level of peer acceptance, with a child's degree of social competence being the best predictor of peer acceptance. Children who are peer-accepted or popular have fewer problems in middle and high school, and teens who are peer-accepted have fewer emotional and social adjustment problems as adults.[1]

---

[1] References: Read more: Peer Acceptance–Antisocial Behavior, Children, and Child–JRank Articles http://psychology.jrank.org/pages/477/Peer-Acceptance.html#ixzz3OT8zsg3C

The choices I made were my choices and I take full responsibility for them, but knowing the lack of peer acceptance could be a small contributing factor to why my thought process was the way it was, is somehow comforting. The biggest struggle we all have is feeling like there is something inherently wrong with us and we are somehow defective, more so than others. So there was some modicum of comfort in feeling like maybe it was not all my fault.

Why I was not accepted in my early childhood is still a mystery to me, but I know I struggled every day of my life toward acceptance and not rejection. Even though I believe peer acceptance was a factor, I have these nagging thoughts to try to explain why I felt the need to chase after these feelings when I had such a stable home and a family who loved me and who would do anything for me. I did not come from a broken home. My parents are still married today, going on thirty-eight years. They supported me through all of my ideas and desires growing up. They came to a lot of my games and cheered for me in the stands. They supported me through the Miss Teen California pageant my freshman year in high school by taking me to all of the interviews and flying me to Southern California for the weekend. They did everything they could for me that they thought would help me grow and to find my identity. They would not allow me to do things they knew would stunt that growth. They were my parents. My siblings and I fought a lot growing up, but we also had a lot of good times. Looking in from the outside, I imagine we would be the stable family that people would want to join. However, I started to brush my family aside in my teen years to go off on a path that would forever change my life.

My senior year in high school, I started to rebel against my parents. I would make up any excuse not to go to church. The need to be part of the popular crowd began to take over. While I was in sports, I did everything I needed to do to make sure I could play in the games. Once I played my last game, I felt an even bigger void in my life that I tried to fill. By the time basketball was over, I only had a few more months until I graduated. I started to hang out with my friends more and going to parties. These friends liked to drink and smoke. They had the freedom that I never had. I would lie to my parents to go out to these parties and I began to drink more and more. I was part of the cool crowd, and that was what filled my sense of loss. Knowing you will never play the one thing that you love the most brings a depression and sense of loss that can overtake you. I felt like I had no idea who I was or what I would do. I was seventeen and completely lost. Sports had become my identity and when that was over, I needed a new identity. I had no idea who I was or what I wanted. More importantly, I had lost the vehicle of popularity that signaled acceptance from my peers.

When it comes to personalities, I am definitely my father's daughter, which is why I believe my relationship with my dad suffered the most at this time. We argued constantly. I wanted to go to cosmetology school instead of four years of college and we fought about that. I wanted to do things that went against the plans my parents had for me and we fought about that. I was tired of all of the rules and boundaries my parents had set for me. I felt completely claustrophobic. I wanted to be free and follow the beat to my own drum and not anyone else's. My parents would give me ultimatums and I rebelled against those. I was rude to my siblings and treated them with rejection. Nothing would stand in the way of me finding myself my own way, with the exception of going to the four-year college. That was the one thing I agreed to do. I could at least move out. As long as I finished school, my parents would pay for it, which I realize now was such an amazing opportunity for me as I know many people do not get that same privilege. I was accepted to two state colleges, Chico and San Diego State, both on the top ten list of party schools. I chose to go to San Diego State and promptly moved to the opposite end of the state from my family. Here I thought I would go to school, hurry up and get my degree, and start my career. Little did I know it would be the start of a dark path over the next few years.

Chapter 2

The Dark Path Begins

———— ✳ ————

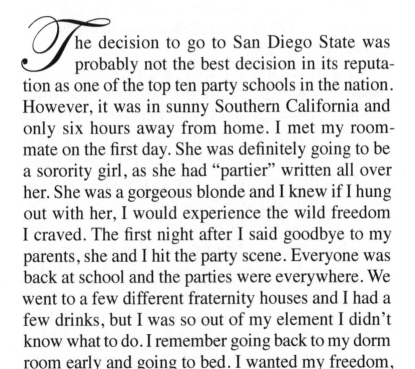he decision to go to San Diego State was probably not the best decision in its reputation as one of the top ten party schools in the nation. However, it was in sunny Southern California and only six hours away from home. I met my roommate on the first day. She was definitely going to be a sorority girl, as she had "partier" written all over her. She was a gorgeous blonde and I knew if I hung out with her, I would experience the wild freedom I craved. The first night after I said goodbye to my parents, she and I hit the party scene. Everyone was back at school and the parties were everywhere. We went to a few different fraternity houses and I had a few drinks, but I was so out of my element I didn't know what to do. I remember going back to my dorm room early and going to bed. I wanted my freedom, but I was definitely outside the bubble I had lived in for so many years—that bubble my parents and I had

created growing up. It was a whole different world full of kids my age and it was the first time we were on our own. It was about to get crazy.

The next day, my roommate told me she met a bunch of guys at the fraternity house across from our dorms and we were all going to the beach. It was a great day and I made a lot of friends. It was also the start of a downward spiral that would take me years to overcome. I would go to all of their parties and hang out with them on different nights. We were their "girls." I would get drunk every night and miss class half of the time. School was definitely not a priority in my life.

With the desire for love and acceptance I so craved, I began to look for that special relationship. The one thing I thought I would preserve until marriage, my virginity, I ended up giving up one night while completely intoxicated. Over the next week, I realized the man I gave it up to had no interest in me or a relationship. He wanted to have fun. The sad part? I was more disappointed he didn't like me enough to be in a relationship, rather than the loss of my virginity. Even more sad? I got over it quickly and turned to the next person who started to show interest in me, and then on to the next person and on to the next person. Everyone I met was connected to this fraternity house. I soon had a reputation of the girl who was easy. Growing up I never wanted to be "that girl," but that is what I became.

I wanted love so badly, I was willing to give up the things that would give me a great man and a lasting love. I gave up my integrity, my respect, and my dignity. The love I searched for was a forever type of love. I wanted to settle down, have kids, and live the normal life with a family of my own, but I would never get there by disrespecting myself and disrespecting God.

I read a book called *Lady in Waiting* a couple of years ago and it stated:

> Too many women grow up believing that the inconsolable ache in her heart is for "a man." To love a man, get married, and then have children is thought to be the only script that will satisfy her heart's deepest longing. But no man, woman, or child can appease this longing; it can only be satisfied by the ultimate Bridegroom, Christ Jesus. *Lady in Waiting* is not about finding the right man, but being the right woman.

I will talk more about this later in the book, but the point is, at this time in my life I was far from the mark of where God wanted me to be.

During this time I started to get depressed. I still had this void I tried to fill. I didn't want to go to class; I didn't know what I wanted to do with my life. I would sleep all day and then get up and go to parties and drink until I stumbled home or threw up and passed out on bathroom floors. Hangovers were an almost everyday thing. Part of me wanted to curl up and not wake up again. As you can guess, the first semester I was at school, I was put on academic probation for my grades. It made sense; I wanted to sleep and drink all night, not be responsible, wake up, and go to class.

The probation was a bit of a wakeup call. My second semester my roommate moved into her sorority's house. I had the dorm room all to myself and I quickly became friends with a different group of people. By this time I went to class a little bit more, but more out of fear of what my parents would do if I was kicked out of school. I wanted to get a job so I had my own money to go out and do different things. My parents told me no. They did not want me to work so I could focus on school. I went out and got a job anyway. I liked having my own money, so I worked a little bit more than part time. I was good at my job and it started to take some of the depressive thoughts away, but I still went out and drank way too much.

My new group of friends was my Navy friends I met in Tijuana, Mexico in a club one night. This helped me to stop going to all of the fraternity parties, which took me out of that scene, but I didn't learn anything. This group also loved to drink and I took the bad habits and decisions I made and redirected it to them. On the weekends we would get together and play drinking games. My focus was still not on school, but on partying with my friends. Although I went to more classes, I hardly studied and I did not do well on tests. By the time my first year was over, I had failed some of my classes and my probation became a reality. I was no longer accepted at San Diego State. I was kicked out of college. Who would have thought I would have drifted so far off the path my parents wanted for me? Normal kids who had the opportunity to go to college would have at least had the responsibility and discipline to get through four years of school, even if they did go out and have a little fun.

So there I was: kicked out of school and didn't about what I would do in my future. I was lived in the moment. I had a job I loved and a group of friends I liked to hang out with and drink. My best friend and I wanted to move into an apartment off campus. Living in the dorms was an experience, but not something you necessarily wanted to do for more than a year and I did not have a choice. It was time for us to spread our wings a little more. I was able to talk my parents into helping out with the rent as long as I enrolled in a junior college to continue taking classes and to get back on track. I was focused on improving my life and getting it back on track. Clearly that was not the case. However, I did have an apartment of my own, a job where I made my own money, and a little more freedom.

My time with my Navy friends drifted off as I broke up with the guy I briefly dated and a new group of friends came into play. They were a group of people I looked up to. They were cool and awesome. They liked me and I felt part of something. We had a lot of house parties where only the group of close friends would be able to climb up on top of the roof and look down at about two hundred people in the backyard all having a blast. I enjoyed that time. I felt genuinely befriended more with this group of friends than I did with all my friends my first year of college. It was this group of friends who eventually got me into using ecstasy. I was okay with drinking heavily, but I never thought I would do what I considered "hard core" drugs. I also smoked marijuana a few times a week, but I thought that was okay and that was the limit. However, that strong relationship I had with this group of friends made me want to do whatever they did.

I wish I could say I hated the feelings that came along with the use of ecstasy, but I didn't. I loved it. For someone who constantly seeks love and attention, this was the perfect drug. It is what we used to call, "the love drug." Everything you touched made you feel wanted and welcomed. It brought our friendships closer and it was an out of this world feeling. In fact, I used ecstasy so much, I found I had to take double the dose to get that same high. I wanted that feeling over and over again and I wanted to be part of the cool crowd. We would go to raves and have rave parties at home where we would have about twenty or thirty people over. I felt on top of the world. The problem was when I came off the drug, reality set in. I would have to go to school and work, and I still didn't have a steady boyfriend. I was definitely not close to my family as I had pushed them as far away from me as I could. I felt alone. I started to feel more and more depressed when I was sober, so I would continue to drink, smoke marijuana, and take ecstasy pills. The more I didn't have to deal with reality, the better. I was so far from God and so lost and yet, I continued to go deeper down into a muddy pit.

I still looked for love in all the wrong places, and there wasn't a prospect in sight. My life consisted of absolutely nothing of value. I couldn't even tell you who I was or what I wanted at that point. I still tried to find my way. My parents could do nothing right. My moods were all over the place. I think if I had seen a psychiatrist, they could have diagnosed me with being bipolar, but looking back, it was the drugs. I would be happy one moment, depressed the next, and then angry if something didn't go right. No wonder no one wanted to date me long term. I thought I was cool by doing drugs and drinking. I was actually proud I was able to hold my alcohol better than most people. Yet, the reality was I was not the person I wanted to be and I was not the person a man deserves to have as a girlfriend. During all of this, I constantly thought about change. What could I do to change my circumstances, but still have control over the direction? I didn't want to go home; that would admit that I failed. There was no way that would happen.

As I write this and going through the timeline of my life, I can't help but relate to Alice in Wonderland. As she went through the different challenges she faced in chasing the white rabbit, she chose to take pills, drink liquids, and eat different cakes to change her size to be able to fit through different doors and to get to where she needed to go. That so applies to my life. I would meet different groups of people and I would conform myself and my personality to fit that setting so I would be accepted. Exactly how Alice had no idea where she was headed, neither did I. We both blindly followed the curiosity of the circumstances in front of us to find we were in a world we did not know. I created my own *Alice in Wonderland,* full of mad hatters, potions, mushrooms, and all the other wonderland items so I could find love and feel accepted. At that time of my life, I had no idea where to go. I didn't think in the long term, only what would give me that temporary satisfaction.

"Would you tell me, please, which way I ought to go from here?"

"That depends a good deal on where you want to get to."

"I don't much care where—"

"Then it doesn't matter which way you go."

- Lewis Carroll, *Alice in Wonderland*

The problem is it should always matter which way we go, as the decisions we make have either blessings or consequences that more often than not impact other people.

Those who live according to the flesh have their minds set on what the flesh desires; but those who live in accordance with the Spirit have their minds set on what the Spirit desires. The mind governed by the flesh is death, but the mind governed by the Spirit is life and peace. The mind governed by the flesh is hostile to God; it does not submit to God's law, nor can it do so. Those who are in the realm of the flesh cannot please God. —Romans 8:5-8

My heart had hardened to the point where it would be hard for me to find my way back to the light. I lived for the flesh of this world and not by the spirit. Instead of stopping to reflect on where I wanted to go, I relied on my spontaneous reflexes and only saw what I wanted at that moment. That was a whole new setting. San Diego was not what I wanted anymore.

My cousin was getting married in Florida at this time and she asked me to be her Maid of Honor. I was so excited to see her and meet all of her friends and to be a part of her special day. So I took a week vacation in Florida. I had a lot of fun getting to reconnect with my cousin and enjoying the life she had built in Florida and the different culture. I met a bunch of people and of course I met a guy I connected with the first day there. I didn't think it would go anywhere since I lived in California, but I had so much fun, I quickly decided to move there. I remember writing my parents a letter to tell them I was dropping out of school and moving to Florida to be on my own. I knew they wouldn't approve and I wanted to make sure I got everything I had to say out in the open without them trying to talk me out of it. I wrote the letter and I think they were speechless for a few minutes.

Courtney told her mother and I about her desire to drop out of school and move to Florida. We were pretty frustrated with her. She wanted to quit just 6 weeks from completing her 2nd year. We asked her to please finish out the year and then leave. At least she would have 2 years completed of college. But little did we know that she had not only failed her first year, but was also failing her second year. She was running away from her problems and she could not bear to tell us the truth. We had to let her go. We made sure she understood though that her decision would eliminate any future support to go back to school. In hindsight, her situation was desperate for her...and she left. As parents, we were frustrated and extremely concerned.

It wasn't only about me moving to Florida, but it was about me cutting myself off from my parents, their money, and dropping out of school. I needed to go find myself and I needed to do it on my own. At least that is what I tried to convince myself of. In reality, I wanted a whole new set of friends who would love and accept me and there was a whole new pool of men that would increase my chances to find true love. So I quit my job, sold some of my possessions, and I moved to Florida with thirty dollars in my pocket. I was excited for a whole new change and to get my life in order. I was in control now, not my parents, and I would be responsible for my own decisions.

Little did I know I would go down a path darker than anything else I had known in the last couple of years. I was Alice and I fell in the rabbit hole where I continued to fall. The light at the top of the rabbit hole got smaller and smaller until I finally hit rock bottom and my efforts to stand back up while in pure darkness would be the hardest thing I would ever do.

It (the human spirit) had turned from God and become its own idol, so that though it could still turn back to God, it could do so only by painful effort, and its inclination was self-ward. Hence pride and ambition, the desire to be lovely in its own eyes and to depress and humiliate all rivals, envy, and restless search for more, and still more, security, were now the attitudes that came easiest to it....A new species, never made by God, had sinned itself into existence.–C.S. Lewis

Chapter 3

The Lost Daughter

————— ✳ —————

He also said: A man had two sons. The younger of them said to his father, "Father, give me the share of the estate I have coming to me." So he distributed the assets to them. Not many days later, the younger son gathered together all he had and traveled to a distant country, where he squandered his estate in foolish living. After he had spent everything, a severe famine struck that country, and he had nothing. Then he went to work for one of the citizens of that country, who sent him into his fields to feed pigs. He longed to eat his fill from the carob pods the pigs were eating, but no one would give him any. When he came to his senses, he said, "How many of my father's hired hands have more than enough food, and here I am dying of hunger!" —Luke 15:11-17

The story of the prodigal son is a famous story that many of us can relate to in some way. Our self-centered nature can take over and drive us down paths of destruction that will bring us to our knees. The only problem is a lot of the time we do not realize it is a destructive path until we are too far down it. We look back and try to figure out how we got to that point in our life. Like the prodigal son making one bad decision after another, I was the lost daughter who did not want or need any help. I wanted to live life to the fullest. So I did, right into the bowels of darkness—a deep void filled with crack and cocaine.

Who knew that the girl who grew up in a Christian home with strong moral values would end up almost destroying her life? This girl went from being a star athlete in high school to wild drinking and using drugs, to a crack house in Florida. Yet, God knew, and I know now, He allowed me to go through some hard times so He could use me. I look back on my time in Florida and know without a shadow of doubt God had His hand upon me through every moment. He would not let me plunge completely down a path from which I could not return.

The first night in Florida was exciting: a new place, new friends, and most of all—new love prospects. I immediately started dating someone. However, I quickly found out that occasionally he liked to smoke crack and snort cocaine. Of course I wanted to be the cool girlfriend, so I followed suit.

How I made the jump from drinking too much to smoking crack for the first time is somewhat of a mystery to me. It happened so fast. Yet, God had a plan for me, but I wouldn't know it for a few years.

People always say hindsight is 20/20 and believe me—I can vouch for that. Looking back I see God's hand in every situation in which I put myself. I made choices that make me cringe at the thought of God's reaction. I turned away from Him and I can only imagine the hurt and disappointment as He turned me over to the wants of my hardened heart. Yet, He spared me death, He spared me jail, and so many other scenarios that could have been even worse. He showed me unconditional love even when I tried so hard not to know Him. Florida ended up being my tornado state. The time in my life where I spun full speed in circles and caused destruction left and right, which included destruction to my family, my friends, and myself.

I lived with my cousin for a little while, and then eventually started dating someone else and moved in with him, continuing my downfall. Most nights, we sat on the patio with neighbors and drank. I had a steady job working at a salon, which sparked my interest to go to cosmetology school so I decided to enroll. Things appeared to be good. I had a man I loved, an apartment, friends, and a good job. I slowly built my life back up again, that is, until my boyfriend stopped paying attention to me. The love that I so needed was not filled anymore and I spun into a more depressive state. I found myself trying every-thing I could to make him continue to love me. We soon ended things; he moved out and I was alone again. I partied more at the bars and ended up deep back into drugs. Instead of doing cocaine maybe once every other week, I did it once a week, then twice a week, then almost every day of the week. I still needed that empty void filled. The void that I thought would be filled by the love and attention of a man. When I did not have it, or felt it was not enough, I tried to numb myself. I was lost.

God wired us to love and to be relational. However, the relationship He designed is the rela-tionship we need to have with Him. If we do not have that relationship with Him, then we have a void in our hearts and we long and search for something to fill it. The problem is no one can fill it except for Jesus Christ. As long as we ignore Him, we will con-tinue to search to fill that void. The void that is made for love and acceptance through Christ will never be filled by friends, family, a significant other, drugs, alcohol, and anything else in this world. Yet, we con-tinue to search for that next thing to make us happy. When the temporary feeling of happiness wears off, we look for that next best thing.

Throughout the first year in Florida, I made a lot of friends. Now looking back, I recognize them more as acquaintances. My desire to continuously find that happiness was almost without a conscious. If friends needed me for something, but it interrupted my plans to go party, I would blow them off so I could do what was on my agenda. Human tendency is to want as many friends as possible. It helps us feel like we mean something in this world. However, we also have to know how to be a true friend in order to keep those relationships. I was not that friend. I wanted everyone to be there for me, but I was so self-centered, I did not return the friendship.

I remember one night a friend's brother was in a car accident and was killed. I had just hung out with him a few weeks prior to the accident, so it was someone I knew. Everyone was getting ready to go over to the family's house to express their condolences, but I had plans to go to a bar. So instead of canceling my plans to be a support for my friends, I simply said I was sorry for their loss and went to the bar. I was so preoccupied with my own selfish wants that I didn't even stop and be that supportive friend. I had no idea how to be a friend, and I got called out on it. My friend, who is the sister of the man who died, said she didn't want anyone at the funeral who couldn't care less that he died and asked I not attend. So as everyone got ready to go to the funeral, I sat crying on my couch with guilt of knowing what I did wrong. How could I be so selfish? It wasn't like I had something important that I couldn't cancel. I went to the bar! This type of behavior quickly turned me into someone I did not want to be, neither was I raised to be. It was the path of destruction that follows a pursuit of false happiness.

When you become addicted to drugs, love, and acceptance, life becomes all about you and not about anyone else. The god of self-interest starts to rear its ugly head and the addictions form a heart of idolatry. It's unfortunate it leaves a path of destruction and a feeling of not being complete, or good enough, or worthy enough of a life on this earth. So what better way to self-protect than rationalize no one else matters except you? You are the only one who is going to make things better for you. No one else is going to help in that, so follow your wants and needs and take control of your life. It doesn't matter who you step on because they don't matter. You are the one who matters. Right? As I would ultimately find out, I was so wrong!

I skipped work on a regular basis. I did not care I left my employer high and dry. I made up excuse after excuse because I was either coming down from a high or I was on one of my cocaine binges. I would disappear for days at a time and did not care who wondered about me. I would tell myself that I had already broken all of the relationships I had, so it didn't matter. The relationships that I built were all based off of drugs and sex. That became the determining factor of my value and my self-worth. Every time I was disappointed with a relationship not working, more of my value would diminish, until I felt almost worthless.

My health went downhill quickly. Not only was I severely depressed, but also I didn't eat. When you are snorting cocaine 24/7, you don't have much of an appetite. My diet consisted of drugs and alcohol and the occasional McDonald's dollar menu cheeseburger (when I could round up enough change out of the couch cushions). I became stick thin. My ribs showed. I had no energy, no motivation, and no nutrition in my body, but I continued to put one foot in front of the other. I was determined to live my life my way and to find my one true love. If I couldn't find him, I would die trying.

I remember one weekend where my friend came into some money and we had an inconceivable amount of cocaine. He wanted to share it with his friends, so we went on a three-day binge and partied like there was no tomorrow. I remember my heart rate would race throughout this time and while talking to someone I just met, my nose started to bleed. God had His hand on me that weekend, because I should have easily overdosed and died. I still can't believe my whole thought process tried to become that cool kid and accepted among the popular crowd. How did I ever come to believe people who constantly did drugs and partied were the cool kids? My identity was wrapped up in thinking there was value in being the one person who people wanted to hang out with all of the time. I honestly believed that would only happen by being seen as the one who was up for anything.

There are many different stories I could tell you, but they all echo the same scenario. I went out, met people, did drugs, got drunk, slept with different men thinking they would love me if I gave them what they wanted, and I woke up the next morning depressed over what I did the night before. Then, I would start the same cycle over again so I wouldn't feel the shame, guilt, and the pain of my past behavior.

After two and a half years in Florida, I had nothing to show for it. I reached the point where I could not handle my life anymore and had serious thoughts that no one would miss me if I were gone. I had suicidal thoughts. I don't remember ever seriously thinking about killing myself. By that I mean I didn't get to the planning stages of actually doing it. I did not even think much of how I would do it. It was more like Satan tried to get me to that point. Pouncing on my fragile state and knowing if he kept pecking at my thoughts and telling me I was nothing, then he could cause some serious damage.

Our thoughts can be one of the most dangerous weapons to ourselves and to others. Metaphorically speaking, it starts with one little thought that can spiral down and end up in a pool of blood. Here is how it works: it starts with remembering what you did last night, then thinking you are a horrible person for doing what you did. This evolves into full-blown guilt and shame, further exacerbated by recognizing you have done this more than once, which only highlights that despicable person inside. *How can anyone love you? You are never going to be able to get past your mistakes. No one will love you now if they know or find out what you have done.* This begs the question: *why are you even here? If you are not here, no one will miss you because you are so horrible. No one will forgive you anyway.* So you make one of two choices: you go deeper into your suicidal thoughts, or you go back out to the bar or the liquor store to wash away those painful feelings and try to forget the memories swimming around in your head.

In this state we almost always think there are only two options. However, I can tell you from experience that there is a third option, and that is falling on your knees and crying out to God to make the bleeding stop. God will show himself to you if you ask Him and if you seek Him. Sometimes, He will orchestrate circumstances that will show Him to you in a way that shakes you up. His design is to move you to an opportunity to cry out and seek Him. One night when I think God knew I was about to go past the point of no return, He spoke to me. He has His own unique way to speak with each of us and often in such a personal way that it touches the heart to the core. For me, He spoke through a song. A song that would forever change my life.

I can still see it in my mind. I was in my apartment on the floor with my back against the stark white wall in my little dining area. I couldn't afford an actual table so it was an empty space. I had my CD player on the floor and the music played and I sang at the top of my lungs. I have had these moments throughout my life where even as a child, I would get into an emotional state and the only thing I could do to control overwhelming emotions was to sing. I had a passion for singing. It wasn't about me wanting attention from singing, it was from overwhelming feelings of depression or loneliness and singing was my release.

So as I sat on the floor with my legs out in front of me and sang at the top of my lungs, there it was: a song I had heard several times before. This time, it spoke loud and clear to me at that moment. The song was "Tourniquet" by Evanescence. I listened to these words over and over again for several hours that night. It talked about being lost and trying to kill the pain. Can God be our tourniquet and stop the bleeding, or is it too late to be saved. God can return us to our salvation.

When you are in a dark place, it is hard to see any sort of light at the end of the tunnel. You see darkness that slowly becomes darker. However, God opened up my ears to the words

Courtney had called us asking to come home. We prayed about it as we had been doing all along. We prayed for discernment and strength. We had made a decision when she left...to practice tough love with her. The most difficult times as parents were during these times of tough love. Is it time to help her? Is it too soon? Would we only continue to enable her? Has she learned and matured? A parent's natural inclination and instinct is to run and rescue their children, to protect them. But we knew there was greater love in helping them to suffer the consequences of their own decisions and to stand on their own feet. But...was it time to step back in and help? Although we did not know the depth of what she had experienced, we felt led to bring her home. She had asked, no begged us, a number of times, to help her and we had said no. Something was different this time. We let her come home.

of this song and it got my attention. It didn't matter how worthless I felt. It didn't matter how much I felt hated and unloved. It didn't matter how much I had messed up in the past, because it is never too late. We are never too lost to cry out to God and ask for His forgiveness and for Him to be our tourniquet. God can stop the bleeding; we only have to believe He can.

I love the lyrics by Evanescense: "My wounds cry for the grave, My soul cries for deliverance, Will I be denied Christ...Tourniquet...My suicide." When we cry out to God from that dark ugly place, our hearts are full of confusion and questions. Physically and mentally we feel like dying, but our soul, the soul God designed for us, cries out for healing. I have come to learn the healing is God's unconditional love. The part of the song, "Tourniquet...my suicide," can be interpreted as a metaphor. When we truly believe God can heal us, He becomes our tourniquet. My suicide is when I made the decision to stop my old ways. The moment I decided to try to turn my life around, I consciously laid my old self to rest and became a new person. My suicide. Never did I think that those two words would have a positive effect on me, but they did.

After listening to this song over and over again, it became clear to me that I wanted a different life. I wanted it desperately. I had always believed in God, but never had that personal relationship with Him. He was always something in the distance that I had a little knowledge of in my head. He was never real and personal to me. I wish I could say I accepted Him in my life and fully surrendered to Him that night, but I didn't. What I did do was to cry out to Him and in that moment, He gave me the strength to call my parents. I cried to them and asked them to bring me home. After lots of prayer on their side, they decided to help bring me home. Unfortunately, I had a lot of medical issues that needed attention, including multiple exploratory surgeries to figure out why I was in a lot of pain, so I wasn't able to go home right away. It took another month or so for me to get that taken care of and for my parents to plan to get me home.

During that month, however, I went back to my old ways. It only took a few days after God gave me that momentary clarity for me to slip back into darkness. The last month was a blur and to this day, I can't remember everything that happened. It was as if I knew my life would change drastically once I was back with my parents. I needed to get everything out before then.

We all have our ups and downs, but it is a process of having those

> *Her mother and I, on our end, did not know what to expect with Courtney. We had outlined the rules for her return. She must immediately look for and get a job. She had limited time to find an apartment to be on her own again. She had agreed to these terms. But we were also relieved at her returning home and planned to welcome her with open arms and be as supportive as we could. But we too, were scared and relying on God's wisdom.*

"God moments" of clarity and seeking Him to Satan using our vulnerability and fragile state to bring us right back down. I went through three different surgeries that month to find out I had a hernia hidden under my bladder, yet I did drugs and drank until right before my surgeries.

My brother flew out to Florida so he could help drive all of my stuff back. I snorted the last of my coke in the bathroom as he rested on the couch before we hit the road. That is how out of my mind I was. Part of me screamed to be rescued, and the other part of me screamed to continue on this path to my death. A huge war waged in me, but God won the first battle. He got my attention a month before, and although it was a short period of time, He saved me by putting things in motion. He saved me by giving me the strength to reach out to my family even though I was full of shame and embarrassment that I couldn't make it on my own. He saved me when I followed through with the decision to pack up my things and head out of Florida with my brother. The emotions I had that day were so out of control, it felt like I was in the middle of a hurricane, but I wasn't in a boat. It felt as if I had been thrown overboard and although I desperately tried to stay afloat, I was drowning and terrified.

The last five years of my life, I ran down a desperate path to find love and acceptance through relationship after relationship, trying to see how many friends I could acquire. The more friends I had, the more my heart felt filled. For five years, I had the independence of making my own decisions and doing what I wanted when I wanted. Now I would live with my parents again. Back to rules, back to being watched, and back to what I thought was trying to be someone I wasn't so I didn't disappoint them. Back to a family I felt deep in my heart did not understand me or could learn to understand me. I was the black sheep. They did not know everything I had been through. They did not know the emotional wreck that would soon land on their doorstep. I felt I would not be able to relate to them and they would not be able to relate to me. All of these feelings of doubt and loneliness came rushing inside of me as I said goodbye to everything I had known for the last several years. I felt like I was headed into the abyss of the unknown. I couldn't tell my parents about all of the drugs I had done, and all of the mistakes I had made, because they would be so ashamed of me.

Not only did I have the emotional battle within, but I fought a physical battle as well. I did drugs almost seven days a week, and when you wreak that much havoc on your body, it soon depends on that havoc. I had my final surgery a week before I left so I had pain pills to help with the withdrawals, but I eventually ran out of those. I honestly thought it would be so easy for me to stop doing drugs. I would cry myself to sleep a lot of the times in that first month I was home. I tried not to show how much I struggled not only physically, but mentally. It was a much harder task than I originally thought, but I had made the decision to change my life, stuff everything down, and put one foot in front of the other and continue forward, leaving my old self behind.

Right when you start to make the tough decisions that are best for you, little things start to happen to try to knock you down. My brother and I were halfway through Texas on our way home and a highway patrolman was headed the opposite way. He decided he wanted to pull us over and so he literally turned around and cut across the highway. As my brother rolled down his window, the patrolmen immediately said he smelled marijuana and ordered both of us to step out of the vehicle so he could search it. Here I was, trying to do the right thing with my life, and now we were pulled over and searched. I had finally made it out of Florida where I should have been arrested several times over, here I was, in the middle of nowhere in Texas and I could have gone to jail. My brother looked at me with that question in his eyes of, "What do you have in here?" I had all of my belongings in boxes in the bed of the truck and no drugs on me whatsoever. I did, however, loan my truck to a friend a week before I left. So the officer separated my brother and I and searched the entire truck, including a thorough search all of the boxes I had in the back. We sat for at least an hour or two in the hot sun with our hearts pounding out of our chest as we wondered what would happen. My friend apparently had dropped a small little bud of marijuana on the floorboard, and that is all the officer found in the search, so after a stern lecture, he let us go.

It goes to show there are no guarantees that going in the right direction means a smooth path. Life will still challenge you in different ways. It is not always fair and I guess that is why some people go off the rails in the first place. God protected me yet again, even when I didn't deserve it. God will continually forgive us as we ask for it, but we will always have to deal with the consequences of our actions, which won't kill us, but will only make us stronger. These experiences cause us to grow into who we are with an identity grounded in Christ.

Like the prodigal son, I left to venture out on my own and I found myself squandering all of my money, my morals, and everything my parents had taught me growing up. Yet, I eventually made it back home. So as the story of the prodigal son continues, the story of the lost daughter continues as well.

I will set out and go back to my father and say to him: "Father, I have sinned against heaven and against you. I am no longer worthy to be called your son; make me like one of your hired servants." So he got up and went to his father. But while he was still a long way off, his father saw him and was filled with compassion for him; he ran to his son, threw his arms around him and kissed him. —Luke 15:18-21

I made it to Southern California where my parents lived, and although there was a lot of work to be done to repair my relationship with them, they forgave me, opened their arms, and let me run home to them with hearts full of love. God saved me again by giving me God-fearing parents who prayed to know when to help me and bring me home. Now it was time for me to put on my "big girl panties" and start to rebuild my life into one that could make my family proud, and a life that could ultimately make me proud. Little did I know I would come to learn it wasn'asnt could make my family proud, and a life that could ultimately make me proud.

Chapter 4

Transition

---— ❊ ———

"Times of transitions are strenuous, but I love them.
They are an opportunity to purge, rethink priorities,
and be intentional about new habits. We can make
our new normal anything we want."
—Kristin Armstrong

*T*ransitions can be difficult as you let go of one
chapter of your life and start the next chapter.
It can be even more difficult when you are finishing
an entire book and trying to rewrite a second novel,
but I was determined. I was done being poor and
a disappointment not only to my family, but also,
more importantly, to myself. So I started on the path
to healing and hopefully creating some measure of
success.

Coming home was difficult. I was an emotional
wreck. Yet, I poured all of that emotional energy

into finding a job. Within the first couple of weeks, I found a temp-to-hire job as an accounting clerk at a mortgage company. I wanted a job, any job, so I could begin to get back on my feet. However, to my surprise and delight, I quickly found I enjoyed accounting. I had always been good at math and I had a lot of varied interests growing up, especially when it came to play time. Normal girls like to play with Barbies, but I liked to play office. My uncle, who had his own business, used to let my siblings and me raid his supply closet when we visited. So I would set up a station and pretend I had an important office job. I guess I should have known accounting was right up my alley.

I started off with a basic job and was only focused on getting stabilized and proving to myself—and others—that I was responsible. What I left in Florida would become a bad dream someday. I was scared. My confidence in who I was and what I should be doing or not doing…had taken a terrible beating. My self-confidence and self-esteem was in the toilet. I wasn't only scared, but I felt a deep down, agonizing kind of embarrassment. You know how every family has a "black sheep"? Well, I felt that was how my family viewed me. I felt like I was a colossal failure on so many fronts and I wasn't sure I would have the strength and stamina to get it back together. I desperately did not want to disappoint my family again.

In spite of my fears, I put one foot in front of the other and on a daily basis I did my best to settle into my new job. I was determined to make something work. The discovery of an affinity and delight in accounting was a Godsend. It had an excitement to it. Until then, I had never felt like I knew what I enjoyed and/or was good at. It was definitely a boost to my self-esteem that I could have some value, even in something as simple as being good at numbers. I vividly remember coming home and excitedly telling my dad about how I thought I had found something that I truly enjoyed. I think he was excited for me as well, but in a cautious way. I can't say I blamed him, because, my track record up to that point had not been stellar. In fact, it had been a real mess. Still, I knew he and my mom supported me in every way.

Over time, I successfully settled into my job and received lots of affirmation from my bosses. The longer I was there, the more confident I became. I also realized the love of accounting and numbers did not go away. It only solidified in my mind that it was a career I wanted to pursue. There was only one problem: I did not have a degree in accounting. I could see if I wanted to advance in the field, I would have to consider going back to school, which terrified me. That was my lack of confidence speaking. I didn't know if I would have the discipline to get through school. My first effort at it (before I dropped out to go to Florida) had me failing miserably. I thought I knew my limitations and I did not want to fool myself. There was the fear of starting something like that and then failing again. I did not want my family and friends to see that again. I didn't think I could emotionally handle the stress of it.

In spite of my fears, I approached my dad and vocalized the idea of going back to school. I wasn't sure how he would react and so was apprehensive about it. I also knew he had made it clear to me when I dropped out of college that if I ever decided to go back again, he would not pay for it. That had been his rule for all of us kids. He would pay for the first four years of college and nothing more. If we did not finish by that time, it was on us. I didn't want him to think I was asking for a handout. This was something I needed to do, if I was going to do it. I needed to prove something to myself.

My talk with my dad went well. He encouraged me to take one class at a time and slowly get back into a pattern and routine. He kept talking about a Bachelor's degree and I kept telling him that I could not even think about that. I had to only think of an AA (at most) and I was not even sure I could handle that. I was scared of the whole process. My confidence was still low and the memories of failing in San Diego and Florida still felt fresh. Still, I decided to start somewhere and see what happened.

So, I enrolled in school for accounting. I decided to start small and found an online Associate's degree program. As I progressed through the first few classes, I remember my dad telling me to keep going and not get discouraged. Pretty soon, taking classes will be a regular, routine part of my schedule and by the time

I turned thirty, I could have my Master's degree. He had already calculated each program and how long it would take me to finish. All I could think of was how overwhelming that sounded. I was prepared to take baby steps first and finish my AA. I had no idea how far I would go, but my dad had a plan.

Just as he had said, the next thing I knew, I had completed my AA. It wasn't so bad and decided I would continue and see if I could get my B.S. in Accounting. The next thing I knew, I had my B.S. The funny thing is, as I achieved each little milestone, my confidence grew, and by the time I turned 31 I had my MBA with an emphasis in accounting. A lot of effort went into working full-time and going to school full-time, but I did it. I even have the school loans to prove it.

Some people think there is no way they can work and go to school, but I am here to tell you that anything is possible if you put your mind to it. Put one foot in front of the other. It is a lot of sacrifice on your free time, but it's a temporary situation. Once you graduate you not only get some of your free time back, but also, you have accomplished something great. Not everyone has the determination to finish a higher education, but when you do, it's the most rewarding feeling. As my dad often said during this process, once you get that degree, no one can ever take it from you. You will have it for your benefit for the rest of your life. So make the short-term sacrifice for the long-term gain.

My career was everything to me during and after my school years. That was my main and sometimes sole focus for the next few years: working and impressing people and moving up in the corporate world. My motto was work hard, then play hard. I would go out on the weekends and drink until I was passed out or throwing up all night and all in the name of having a good time. I still bounced from one relationship to another as I tried to find that perfect love. Lo and behold, I found myself with the same problem I had in Florida, excluding the drugs. I was back on track with work and school, but I still longed for that love and acceptance and searched for it in all the wrong places.

It goes to show you that you can't run from the underlying problem of why you decide to do drugs or drink excessively. It will follow you no matter where you go unless you meet the problem head on. Changing locations or starting something new only masks the underlying emotional insecurities and needs. The decision needs to be made whether or not to make fresh new starts over and over again versus whether you want complete healing and complete freedom. It was clear I needed to make a decision. It was a dead end. I had tried all of the things I thought would make it better and/or satisfy the longing, loneliness, and emptiness in my heart. I desperately wanted the healing and freedom, but the question was: how do I get that healing and freedom?

I found out later on that I wanted complete freedom, but the only way I would get that was through Jesus Christ and fully surrendering my life to Him. As the quote at the beginning of the chapter said, "we get to make it anything we want." We have to choose. It is our decision to grasp onto the transition of this world or the transformation Jesus Christ can give us.

The key words to a full transformation are full surrender. I knew in my head I needed to get back into church. It was the right thing to do, but my heart was not fully surrendered. We have this little issue called "control." We always want to hold on to everything that is happening in our lives and the people around us, because we feel we can make the right decisions. Even when we do give our lives fully to Christ, we give up our burdens and control and lay them at Christ's feet, but then when the timing is not what we think it should be, or how the problem should be solved, then we take it back, and it goes back and forth.

I had a hard time with not feeling like I was in charge of my life and trusting someone I could not see or physically touch. How could I trust someone I have not spent time with and shaken His hand? How can I not worry about situations that directly affect me and trust God knows best? I couldn't get over it, but I continued to go to church and I soon got heavily involved through the kids program. I figured if I kept going and doing what was right, then everything would eventually fall into place, but I soon found out how wrong I was.

During transitions, Satan will try to knock you back down if you show the slightest interest in a relationship with Christ and that is what Satan did to me. Satan took a vulnerable spot in me and my view of the church upside down. I became very bitter towards religion all together.. After being heavily involved in the church I attended at the time, I ended up needing another surgery. This time I had complications and was out of commission for about three months. Not one person from the church or the team I volunteered with called me to see how I was after the surgery or even cared enough to see why I hadn't returned to church after my surgery. I always remembered the pastor talking about involving yourself in the church so you can become part of the church family. He said if you come to church every Sunday and then bolt without becoming involved then you can't expect to feel part of the community a church body provides. Well, I got involved. I was part of three weekend services a month and volunteered the whole weekend and I didn't even get a call after my surgery. A bitter taste was left in my mouth.

So naturally my thoughts went to why am I killing myself, trying to go to church and do what I am supposed to do if no one cares about me? The church is supposed to take care of each other and to love and support one another. Where was the love? Where was the support? I was crushed. So my heart said to forget them and I stopped going to church all together and turned off my heart to the whole church-and-God thing. I tried, right? It didn't work out. It wasn't for me. I was fine in my life. I had a great job. I was on track with school. I had a bunch of friends. I was fine.

I continued on this path of me, myself, and I and Satan capitalized on it. Have you ever felt you are doing great and you are proud of yourself for everything you did? You did it. Sure, you may have had help, but you picked yourself up off of the ground when times were low. You got a new job and career. You enrolled yourself in school. You can pay your own bills and not worry about it. You have great friendships that you maintain. My life was all about my happiness and me. I was comfortable in my life, everything went smoothly, and life was great.

I will never forget watching "God's Not Dead" and Dean Cain's character was with his mother who had Alzheimer's. He was full of arrogance and did not want to be there. He was too good to be somewhere where no one would know he was there, until God spoke through her. She said sometimes Satan will give us great lives so we don't know we are living in a prison cell until it's too late. If our lives are great and we are comfortable, then how are we to know something is wrong or we need Jesus to complete us? This hit home to me because that was me for so long, thinking I was fine on my own, so why search out a faith that seemed ridiculous to me?

It wasn't until a few years later that I started to feel I truly was missing something I could not fill. I had an emptiness to me that I didn't quite understand. It didn't matter what I did to try and fill that void; nothing would work. My mom invited me to the women's luncheons at her church and introduced me to ladies, and that was okay. She invited me to one of her women's retreats with her church and I was uncomfortable the whole time, but I did it for her. God had a different idea. My heart wasn't quite in the right place, but God used my mom to slowly start planting seeds in me. I may have been uncomfortable going to a retreat, but God slowly opened my heart to the idea of possibly going back to church.

Chapter 5

Intangible God

———— ✳ ————

*M*y path so far had been one of separating myself from God through my habitual sins, my negative experiences with church, and my doubts. There were so many questions for which I needed answers, but my main question revolved around trying to believe in an intangible God living in a tangible world. It felt surreal and strange to believe in something I could not see, touch, or feel. Not only was I to believe in this God, but also, I was supposed to fully surrender to Him? I wasn't so sure I was ready to give up the control on my life, even if it wasn't a part of my plan.

We live in a society today where giving in to selfish desires has become the norm. We live in a world where products are advertised in a way that encourages a feeling of entitlement to self-happiness if you buy them. Sex advertisements are the most prevalent through billboards, TV shows, movies, and commercials. What happened to modesty where sexual relations were meant to stay within the home and between two people in a marriage? We live in a world where you are viewed as abnormal if you don't have sex or move in with your significant other before marriage. Commercials advertise and portray alcohol as the ultimate way to not only have a good time, but it is the primary way. TV and movies often portray it as the remedy to deal with stress and pressure. How many times do you see the upset character run to the bottle and gulp down alcohol to calm down? We live in a society where it is okay to give in to our selfish needs as long as it makes us happy and satisfies our immediate need.

My biggest fear to take that step of fully accepting Christ was how my friends would react to all of the changes I would have to make in order to follow Jesus. My thoughts would automatically go to all of the sacrifices that would have to be made instead of what blessings would come my way. The fear of losing my friends drove these thoughts and I truly believe was one of the major obstacles for the long delay in making my decision. I kept telling myself that I wasn't ready. Another obstacle, driven more by my pride, was in my family always asking me about my hesitation, and that perceived pressure caused me to run further away. No one could tell me when I should accept Christ or that I even had to.

Then there was the ultimate question: what would people think of me? I couldn't have people think I'm a Jesus freak who believes in something so intangible and crazy. Believing in someone who claims to have flooded the earth and killed everyone except Noah's family? We are talking about believing in His Son who miraculously fed five thousand people with three loaves of bread and two fish? We are talking about Jesus, who brought someone back to life after death. So many miracles that simply do not feel possible. Then there is the question that if God is such a great God and He is love, why does He allow bad things to happen to good people? That question got me every time.

Have you ever heard the phrase "perception is reality"? This phrase basically means our perception of something, absent contrary facts, creates the reality in which we live, see the world, and make decisions. It contributes heavily to our worldview.

It is important to realize our perception may become our reality, but that doesn't mean it is an accurate, truthful view of life. For example, all of these questions are asked and then God's answers are dismissed as if it's not possible. Not only can we not believe in an intangible God with all of His miracles, but also we will not submit ourselves to an authority we can't see, feel, or touch. We will not surrender to a God who is inconsistent in how He treats people. See how that works?

That perception is wrong and it is not truth. We have been living in a world full of wrong perceptions perpetrated by a secular worldview that does everything it can to separate us from the real truth of God and our purpose here on this earth.

Let me tell you a story; a story that has been told many times at the dinner table to reminisce and laugh. It was the beginning of summer in Tracy, CA. Just about the time when summer is beginning and it starts to feel hot. Northern CA has a dry heat that cracks your skin and chaps your lips. It turns much of the vegetation brown instead of green, and it was not uncommon to see a large piece of tumbleweed rolling across the streets. My family and I lived in a house at the end of a cul-de-sac and it was right before we decided to put in an in-ground pool. In the far corner of the yard was a large patch of dry weeds about three to four feet tall. It was a Saturday morning and all of us kids had on the morning cartoons. My dad opened the sliding glass door from the backyard and yelled "Hey kids! Want to see something really cool?"

Of course all four of us charged out the back sliding glass door and followed my dad. Who doesn't want to see something cool, right? So he brought us over to the corner of the yard and said, "Look over there," and pointed to a place inside the weeds.

"What is it, Dad?" one of us said.

He said, "Look closely; it's a snake! Do you see it?" We all got a little closer, leaned in, and we saw it.

Right in the middle of the weeds was a snake about four feet long.

My dad then said, "I'm going to grab it."

My mom came out and chimed in, "Honey, don't you dare! We don't know if it is poisonous or not. We should just call animal rescue!"

All of our hearts beat out of our chests. We did not want our dad to get hurt if the snake bit him, but secretly, we thought the snake was cool. After some back and forth between my parents, my dad decided to go for it. He slowly reached in, and then quickly grabbed the snake and lifted it out of the grass. The snake squirmed in his hands and my dad tried to get a better grip on the snake. All four of our eyes immediately opened up wide and we scattered in four different directions. My brother and I ran to the back sliding glass door while my sister ran off to the other side of the house and my youngest brother ran off in another direction.

My brother got to the sliding glass door a couple seconds before I did. You would think being a loving, younger brother he would hold the sliding glass door open for me, but he did not. He slammed it shut and then locked the door so I couldn't get in. I slammed against the door, turned around, and realized I had no place to go. My dad was coming my way with the snake in his hands and my brother had locked me out of the house. I was paralyzed with fear. My heart beat wildly and I was scared to death. My dad got up close and I slid down the door as I screamed at the top of my lungs. I ended up in a seated position, trying to cover myself as if putting my hands over my head would save me from this monstrous, poisonous snake. My dad suddenly stopped and I got the courage to look up. He still held the snake and then, he slowly put the snake's head in his mouth. My brother looked out the sliding door with a shocked look and my eyes got big. Then there was silence. No more screaming, only shock on our faces. The snake was not real. My mom got the snake at a nature store and my parents came up with this elaborate plan to trick us.

The point is my perception that day was that the snake was real and I reacted accordingly. My reality that morning was I would die as my dad chased me with a poisonous snake. However, that perception wasn't the truth. The truth was the snake was fake and if I think about it, I am pretty sure my dad would not try to kill me with a snake. I knew my dad loved me. He would not let anything hurt me. Yet, I forgot that in the panic of the moment.

Take a moment for that to set in. I wish it had set in with me as I ran for my life that day. I would have saved myself a lot of humiliation. However, it has created a story my family will forever remember and will be passed down from generation to generation. If my perception at the time was that I viewed being a Christian as more of a sacrifice than a blessing, was that the wrong perception? Was my reality and my knowledge I had at that time the truth? If not, then what is the truth? If I find out what the truth is, will I still make the right decision? I hadn't been so good in that department in my past.

Truth

My pastor once said the most important thing we can do is to be willing to seek the truth and to ask God to show it to us. You may be one of those people who adamantly denies God and say you don't believe in Him. Or, you may be someone who is like I was with questions and doubts. Or perhaps going to church to appease someone else, but with no intention of falling for this whole "God" thing. Wherever you may be, let me ask this question: would you rather research and seek the truth to make sure the decision you are making is accurate? Take the concept of fully understanding all of the Bible issues out of the equation. If you have truly decided you do not want to follow Jesus, are you interested in making sure you have made an informed decision? God's only desire is for you to seek the truth. It doesn't mean you have to know all of the answers, but seek the truth and ask Him to show you that He exists. He will show you. He will guide you along a path to understand His truth. You don't have to be a Bible scholar to get there.

Jesus said, "the truth will set you free."

To the Jews who had believed him, Jesus said, "If you hold to my teaching, you are really my disciples.

Then you will know the truth, and the truth will set you free" (John 8:31-32).

The truth is God's Word. We live in a world where emotions are forefront and often solely used as a guide to how we live our lives. However, we should make decisions not only on our knowledge, but our hearts as well. However, if our hearts and minds are not aligned, then we will make the wrong decision. Often I made the wrong decision and denied myself the blessings God wanted to give me because my mind was not in line with what my heart knew to be the truth. The truth will set us free, but we have to seek it and be open to it. I made the decision too many times to deny living a life for Christ because frankly, I didn't want to follow anyone but myself. I wanted to be in control. Fully surrendering to someone is hard, but surrendering to what I thought was a mythical character is even harder. I constantly searched for more in my life. I did not have that sense of peace, joy, and love. God knocked at my heart the whole time; I needed to open my mind enough to hear Him and give Him a chance to align my heart and my mind to His desires and love.

The truth is God is sovereign and God is love. The Bible gives us a great description of who He is and His character. We may not be able to see Him, but if we open ourselves to the truth, then we open ourselves to changed hearts that will be able to see and experience Him. Sometimes we need to reach out for the truth, even if our feelings tell us differently. The more aligned our heart and mind becomes, the more we seek the truth, the quicker our transformation.

The hardest thing about seeking God and understanding him is we see so much pain and suffering in the world. If God is love, then how can He allow the pain and suffering to happen to so many good people? This is something I couldn't grasp. Have you wondered the same thing? You have so many questions you want answered and especially the one: if God can prevent it, why doesn't He? That doesn't sound like a loving God. So why should we choose to follow a God who allows these things to happen? Well, one answer is we sometimes only focus on the situations that don't appear fair, just, or right. I believe Satan uses this confusion to keep our hearts and minds misaligned. If we focused on all of the good in the world and look for God's hand in that, it would be a different story. To be honest, we may never fully understand God's actions until we see Him in heaven. However, the truth is God will always use every situation for good, no matter what. Can He prevent something bad from happening? Absolutely, and I believe in many cases He does. We may not see it all the time.

God's desire is for us to choose to love and follow Him through the free exercise of our own free will. If He were to force us to follow Him, then what type of relationship would that be? However, there is risk to allowing people to decide what they believe. There will be those who choose to live a life separate from

God and a life of sinful behavior. However, allowing the world to take its natural course often reaps terrible and painful consequences. I can't always say I understand what God allows and doesn't allow. Many times, it appears the pain and suffering far outweighs our human ability to understand what good could possibly come out of certain situations. So there are times when I see something happen and grieve with other people, not only in their suffering, but also in their confusion and cries to God. Why did this have to happen? Why did this or that person have to suffer so much? I do get angry and at times find myself yelling at God in my lack of understanding. However, I also have a conversation with Him and at the end of the day, I have to trust God is in control. One day, He will avenge those who have suffered by punishing the people who need to be punished. It is the realization the ultimate thing we live and hope for is living eternally in heaven with Christ. One day, there will be no more tears and suffering. In the end, the good will outweigh the bad; as we know Christ won when He died on the cross for our sins.

I am old enough and experienced enough to know God always uses bad things for good. We may not always see it right away, but He will use it for good. He allows us to go through different situations so He can use us later to carry out His work and to help others. God allowed me to go through different situations because He knew I would one day help other women become free from their struggles.

Had I not gone through different trials and tribulations throughout my life, I would not be able to help them in a way that would bring them closer to God because I would not be able to relate to them. I would not have an understanding that comes from a heart that has been there.

Another related question—or I should say, statement—comes from an attitude of self-assessment in being a good person; the logic being if I am a good person and God is this great and loving God, how could He not let me into heaven?

The biggest misconception in this world today is people are inherently good. A good example of this are the self-esteem programs in the schools, which emphasize no matter what you do, you are a good person. The message is reinforced: people are born good. The truth is this is an idea born out of the world we live in. It is not conducive to God's Word that clearly states we are born into sin. Sin is anything we do that separates us from a relationship with God. We naturally and often choose to separate ourselves because we are inherently selfish as a result of being born into sin. We want things the way we want them and we will work independently of God to get them.

I remember one day I was with my mom and my little brother in a department store. My brother was about two, which made me nine. I don't remember all of the details, but my brother wanted something from my mom, and she said no. Whatever he wanted, he wanted it so bad he thought if he threw himself on the floor, crying and screaming, my mother would give him what he wanted. He was two, and he wanted what he wanted, no matter what he had to do to get it. I'm sure you see this in malls and different stores where one of the parents says no to the child, and the child does whatever it takes to try to get them to say yes. Sometimes it is throwing themselves on the floor, and sometimes the child tries to more subtly manipulate their parents to get their way. Either way, human nature is selfish and sinful as evidenced at these early ages, which is more evidence to support God's Word that we are not born inherently good, but into sin. It is then the choice of our free will when we get old enough to understand to choose to follow Christ.

God's grace is free. It is a gift to us. We do not have to work for our salvation. We do not have to earn His forgiveness and grace through good works. The day that Jesus died on the cross was the day that anyone who believes in Him will be forgiven and His grace will cover their sins—past, present, and future. We don't have to earn it, but we do have to make the conscious choice to live for Christ.

"For God so loved the world that he gave his one and only Son, that whoever believes in him shall not perish but have eternal life." —John 3:16

The gospel is simple; however, sometimes we get in our own way and make it unnecessarily complex. That is in part due to our lack of understanding of the Almighty God in comparison to the small world in which we live. Yet, due to God's incredible mercy and grace, as I began to seek answers and open my heart to the possibility that God is the answer, He answered.

"Here I am! I stand at the door and *knock*. If anyone hears my voice and opens the door, I will come in and eat with that person, and they with me." —Revelation 3:20

Chapter 6

Rescued

"Blessed are they whose transgressions are forgiven, whose sins are covered. Blessed is the man
whose sin the Lord will never count against him."
—Romans 4:7-8

*S*ome of my favorite movies are about natural disasters. There is something about the
intensity of a movie and the realization of what could
happen that pulls me in, so my mom introduced
me to Joel Rosenberg, one of my all-time favorite
authors. He writes fiction and non-fiction about current issues, especially throughout the Middle East
and ties them into biblical prophecy. His books are
fascinating to read and within the first few minutes
of me reading his first book, I was hooked with the
intensity he provided. Reading about the end times

and tying it with modern culture made me realize it was a time I did not want to live in.

I always thought I would be able to live my life the way I wanted to live it and then swoop right in to accept Jesus right before the finish line. What was I thinking? We don't know when Jesus will come back and we have to be ready. I can't wait until the end because what I think could be the end may be too late. My mind spun and my heart opened more and more to the idea of following Jesus as I read this series. After I was done, I was onto the *Left Behind* series. I couldn't read enough about the tribulation, the rapture, and everything happening currently, and then it happened. The moment arrived when God got my attention.

The way God grabs hold of our attention is unique to every individual. For one person, it may be a tragedy. For another person, it may be a family member dragging them to church only to hear God speaking to their heart. My point is everyone is different and I was no exception. God used trumpets with me.

Revelation 8:6 says, "Then the seven angels who had the seven trumpets prepared to sound them." I always equated trumpets with Jesus coming back, especially in reading about the tribulation and the biblical prophecies that tie in with the end times. So what happened next was a jaw-dropping moment for me.

I was on my couch on a bright sunny day. It was one of those days where I opened up all of the curtains and windows to feel the sunlight and feel the crisp air as a small breeze flows through the apartment. I was content on my couch, reclining my feet. I had the TV on in the background and I read one of the books from the *Left Behind* series. At the time, I lived across the street from the Crystal Cathedral in Orange, CA, a church known for their architecture and services. All of a sudden, I heard the sound of trumpets. This was not any normal sound of trumpets, but a trumpet sound loud enough to shake my apartment walls. I immediately jumped up, and I tried to push down my recliner at the same time. I almost tripped over it because the recliner didn't close all the way and it popped right back up and hit the back of my legs, but it didn't matter because I was in straight panic mode. I breathed heavily and my heart pounded. I literally thought I might be having a heart attack, except my pure fear and panic was caused from thinking I was left behind. That's right; I thought the trumpets blew and the rapture had happened and I had dragged my feet on making a decision to surrender my life to Christ.

I immediately called my mom because if she answered, then there was no way the rapture had happened. She would be one of the first people standing next to Jesus, and of course my mom is one of those people who doesn't always have her phone easily accessible. She normally has it at the bottom of her purse or she forgot where she put it. So she took awhile to answer the phone. I was in sheer panic mode, while she was probably nonchalantly digging through her purse, trying to find her phone. Then she finally answered. A weight lifted off of my shoulders I didn't realize was there and I immediately said, "Good you are still here!" Of course she had no idea what I meant, so I told her, talking a mile a minute, and all she could do was laugh. However, the anxiety and fear I felt for that small moment was enough to scare the daylights out of me. I no longer wanted to wait to accept Christ, so I did it right then and there. Granted, as you know I accepted Christ when I was eleven, but I did not fully surrender my life to Christ, which is a tremendous difference. This time it was full surrender.

I no longer wanted to be in charge of my life. I had already made enough of a mess with it. I needed someone who loved me unconditionally. I needed someone who knew what was best for me even when I couldn't figure it out for myself. I needed someone who could forgive me for my past sins—and there was a lot to forgive—and to say, "It doesn't matter because you are my child and I love you." I needed God and I finally found "something" that would fill the emptiness I felt in my heart. I was now complete. The one thing I needed all of those years was right next to me at every moment and whispered in my ear, "I am right here; you have to seek me."

By the sound of trumpets God got my attention and He rescued me. The peace and joy I felt was overwhelming. A dark mist had hung over my head and as time went on, that dark mist kept getting darker and thicker and was slowly starting to suffocate me. Part of me knew something was not right, but I could not quite put my finger on it and so the darkness overwhelmed me until Jesus rescued me. When I made the decision to fully surrender myself to Christ, it was like that thick dark mist evaporated into thin air and I could breathe again. I breathed fresh crisp mountain air with no toxic pollution and I was on cloud nine. My desire to follow Christ was on fire. I went to church regularly and listened to the sermons. What was next? I didn't know what was expected of me as a new child of God. I knew it wasn't enough to go to church regularly and I had so much to learn. God slowly began to show me the areas of my life I needed to change. It wasn't about learning more about Jesus; it was about making changes in my life and applying the knowledge I gained.

God will always reveal things to you that need work. A special sermon will convict you in a certain way or He will lay something on your heart. For me, I was on fire for God, but still tried to live my life the way that I had always lived it. I had been in complete control of my life for so long, it was all I knew how to do. That was the problem—I had lived my life independent of God. I didn't incorporate God into my life. For so long, it had been all about me, so even though I went to church and wanted to learn and read my Bible, I needed to change even more. The old activities I used to do slowly began to lose their appeal. It was not as much fun. God convicted me and transformed my heart over time as I still indulged my old life and friends. Even though I had changed and committed my life to Christ, it is still hard to go cold turkey on your friends and old habits. However, over time, I found going out and drinking excessively was not much fun anymore. It took me longer to recover from the hangovers and I found it didn't have the same meaning for me as it used to.

Going from one boyfriend to the other and sleeping with them didn't work anymore. I found myself wanting to find a man who went to church and had the same values. The men I used to date were not emotionally attractive to me anymore. God opened up my eyes to how I should be treated from a biblical perspective and how I deserved to be treated as His child. Intimacy was something special to be shared between a man and a woman within the confines and commitment of marriage. A few months after I fully surrendered my life, I made the decision to wait until I got married to once again experience that intimacy. I made the choice to change my outlook on dating and to completely revamp my idea of what I wanted in a man and a relationship.

This led me to transform how I dressed. God opened my heart to the idea of modesty. It was something I had never seriously considered. In today's world, it is okay and encouraged to wear low-cut shirts that reveal cleavage, and short shorts. The sexier, the better. Your identity becomes wrapped up in how you look on the outside and always wanting to adapt to the trends of the materialistic society in which we live. For many years, I had no problem going along with this conception. However, in my newfound commitment to Christ, I felt self-conscious. The clothing I bought was still fashionable, but covered more of my body.

It's amazing to look back to see how much God transformed my life in different areas. What I once thought was okay and normal was the complete opposite of what I now know to be right in the eyes of God. In the transformation, God completely changed my desires. I never thought I could change this much, but with God, anything is possible. Little by little, God showed me different things He wanted me to work on. I am a continuous work in progress. Unfortunately, I don't always hear Him until He knocks the wind out of me or pulls the rug from underneath me. A few years back, about a year after my decision to live for Christ, He did exactly that. God rescued me when I accepted Him into my life, but He rescued me again when He showed me what I needed to work on: my past.

God had already forgiven me of my past sins and I mean *all* of my sins, but I have also come to believe He wants us to learn from our past mistakes. So, even though He has forgiven our sins and forgotten them, there is value at times to revisit our past to understand the whys of the choices and decisions made at the time. How else are we going to learn from it and grow? I understand it is desirable to acknowledge our past and then forget it. Many memories are painful and embarrassing. However, God wants to be able to use all bad things for good, so there is a process for Him to be able to use someone to do His work. We have to know and understand we are broken and why we're broken in order for God to rebuild us in His image and in His character. It's amazing how God gets my attention each time. Once it was trumpets from the Crystal Cathedral and now it was a major neck surgery.

For two years, I had neck pain and upper back spasms. There were times when I would wake up and not be able to lift my neck without shooting pains going down my left arm and the left side of my back. I constantly had headaches and was in excruciating pain. At first I thought it was related to working at a desk at work. I would sit in front of a computer all day—sometimes ten hours a day—and my poor posture did not help. I went often to the doctor to get prescriptions for Vicodin and muscle relaxers. This would alleviate the flare-ups for a short time, only to go through it again a month later. After approximately two years of this, I felt weakness in my left arm and tingling in my fingers. So I told the doctor that I needed to be referred to a specialist. He agreed and prescribed an MRI and a visit to the Brain and Spine Institute. Within a minute of the doctor seeing my MRI, he diagnosed me with a degenerative bulging disc between my C5 and C6 cervical (neck) vertebrae. He said it had been many years since he had encountered this level of trauma in someone under forty. I was thankful something was actually wrong and it wasn't my imagination, but at the same time, I was scared to death that I now needed neck surgery. He wanted to get it done within the next three weeks.

Up to this point, I had been on pain medication for several weeks so by the time of the surgery, I had been on pain medication for a total of six weeks. The surgery came and went and I was in a lot of pain for the first four weeks after surgery. I took double the dose of pain medication every four to five hours so I would not risk the pain getting too severe. I pushed myself to be back at work in three weeks, but I would need to be in a neck brace for a total of six weeks. After six weeks, I was to go through physical therapy to try to get the strength back in my neck and shoulder muscles. Everything was going to according to plan until I was out of pain medication. I decided I didn't need it anymore so I threw the bottle away. Within the first eight hours I started to feel under the weather and twenty-four hours later, I went through physical withdrawals, although I did not recognize it at first. I never wanted to think about withdrawal again, let alone have it be the worst withdrawal I had ever been through. Initially, I started to shake or tremble a little and I couldn't focus. My head pounded and my whole body itched and at times and felt like it was on fire. My stomach was in knots, my hands were clammy, and food did not digest properly. The worst part was not being able to get warm. I was so cold. At first, I did not put two and two together, but then I realized I had become addicted to the pain medication. I went to my boss and explained everything. Luckily, she was under-standing, told me to call the doctor, and sent me home with the admonition to take the next day off.

I immediately went home and called the doctor. They could not believe I had stopped cold turkey with my medications. They told me it was dangerous to do that and I needed to gradually wean myself off of the medication. So they called in another pre-scription and gave strict instructions on how many to take each day until I didn't need to take anymore. The hour between when I called and took the next pill was extremely hard for me. I felt like a junky who could not wait for the next fix. Then it hit me like a semi-truck. All of the feelings I had from years ago and the things I did—doing drugs and drinking— came crashing into my brain at two hundred miles an hour. I felt like a computer who processed infor-mation too fast and was ready to blow up. I fell to my knees sobbing while rocking back and forth as I tried to gain back control.

The rush of guilt and shame for everything I had done hit me like a ton of bricks and for the first time, I felt the weight of my past actions on my shoulders. It wasn't only bad decisions anymore as I had con-vinced myself over time. Now that I was a Christian, it was the weight of my sinful actions and what I had done, not to myself, but to Jesus Christ. It wasn't only living with the consequences I had brought upon myself, it was realizing the full impact it had on everyone around me. I fully began to understand my past actions.

My brain raced at warp speed and my heart ached so bad I thought I would have a heart attack. The emotional pain manifested itself into physical pain and I couldn't stop crying. It was one of those ugly cries where you can't breathe and you can't catch your breath. God was once again getting my attention and in a big way. I didn't know what was going on and it would take some time to make sense of it. Unfortunately there is 20/20 vision in hindsight, right? My first thought was to call my mom. She somehow always knew what to say and most of what she said made me feel better, but some of it felt convicting. Clearly she was God's messenger. I don't think she fully understands even to this day that the words she said to me that day paved the way for the work the Lord wanted me to do and how impactful it was for me. They weren't only words of wisdom, but words that would completely change the course of my life.

I called crying so hard I could barely talk. With patience, she finally got out of me what was wrong and as she pieced together what had happened, she proceeded to tell me that Satan was pissed off I had a real relationship with Christ. He tried to get at me in any way possible to throw me off track and he had some success. He tried hard to take this moment to make me feel as worthless as possible. His goal was to put doubts in my head and heart about what Christ had done for me. I thought, *after everything I had done, how could God love me*? How could anyone love me? I had hurt so many people, it would be better to distance myself because apologizing wouldn't be good enough.'

At that moment, I had a choice to make: to believe the lies going through my head or cry out to God. God sent me His Word and the strength I needed through my mother. She calmed me down by telling me God is going to use this experience for His work; He can't begin to use any of us until we are broken and more importantly, that we understand that we are broken. Well, I was broken at that moment.

Over time, God opened my eyes to 2 Samuel Chapter 22. I read it over and over again until it was ingrained into me as to who was my rock. I still read it to this day and give out to other people who need encouragement.

David sang to the Lord the words of this song when the Lord delivered him from the hand of all his enemies and from the hand of Saul. He said:

The Lord is my rock, my fortress and my deliverer; my God is my rock, in whom I take refuge, my shield and the horn of my salvation. He is my stronghold, my refuge and my savior-from violent people you save me. I called to the Lord, who is worthy of praise, and have been saved from my enemies. The waves of death swirled about me; the torrents of destruction overwhelmed me. The odds of the grave coiled around me; the snares of death confronted me. In my distress I called to the Lord; I called out to my God. From his temple he heard my voice; my cry came to his ears. The earth trembled and quaked, the foundations of the heavens shook; they trembles because he was angry. Smoke rose from his nostrils; consuming fire came from his mouth, burning coals blazed out of it. He parted the heavens and came down; dark clouds were under his feet. he mounted the cherubim and flew; he sordid on the wings of the wind. He made darkness his canopy around him- the dark rain clouds of the sky. Out of the brightness of his presence bolts of lightning blazed forth. The Lord thundered from heaven; the voice of the Most High resounded. He shot his arrows and scattered the enemy, with great bolts of lightning he routed them. The valleys of the sea were exposed and the foundations of the earth laid bare at the rebuke of the Lord, at the blast of breath from his nostrils. He reached down from on high and took hold of me; he drew me out of deep waters. He rescued me from my powerful enemy, from my foes, who were too strong for me. They confronted me in the day of my disaster, but the Lord was my support. He brought me out into a spacious place; he rescued me because he delighted in me. The Lord has dealt with me according to my righteousness; according to the cleanness of my hands he has rewarded me. For I have kept the ways of the Lord; I am not guilty of turning from my God. All his laws are before me; I have not turned away from his decrees. I have been blameless before him and have kept myself from sin. The Lord has rewarded me according to my righteousness, according to my cleanness in his sight. To the faithful you show yourself faithful, to the blameless you show yourself blameless, to the pure you show yourself pure, but to the devious you show yourself shrewd. You save the humble, but your eyes are on the haughty to bring them low. You, Lord, are my lamp; the Lord turns my darkness into light. With your help I can advance against a troop; with my God I can scale a wall. As for God, his way is perfect: The Lord's word is flawless; he shields all who take refuge in him. For who is God besides the Lord? And who is the Rock except our God? It is God who arms me with strength and keeps my way secure. He makes my feet like the feet of a deer; he causes me to stand on the heights. He trains my hands for battle; my arms can bend a bow of bronze. You make your saving help my shield; your

help has made me great. You provide a broad path for my feet, so that my ankles do not give way. I cursed my enemies and crushed them; I did not turn back till they were destroyed. I crushed them completely, and they could not rise; they fell beneath my feet. You armed me with strength for battle; you humbled my adversaries before me. You made my enemies turn their backs in flight, and I destroyed my foes. They cried for help, but there was no one to save them- to the Lord, but he did not answer. I beat them as fine as the dust of the earth; I pounded and trampled them like mud in the streets. You have delivered me from the attacks of the people; you have preserved me as the head of nations. People I did not know now serve me, foreigners cower before me; as soon as they hear of me, they obey me. They all lose heart; they come trembling from their strongholds. The Lord lives! Praise be to my Rock! Exalted be my God, the Rock, my Savior! He is the God who avenges me, who puts the nations under me, who sets me free from my enemies. You exalted me above my foes; from a violent man you rescued me. Therefore I will praise you, Lord, among the nations; I will sing the praises of your name. He gives his king great victories; he shows unfailing kindness to his anointed, to David and his descendants forever.
—2 Samuel 22 (NIV)

I called out to the Lord and He saved me. He proved to me that day and over the next couple of days that no matter what happens, no matter what Satan does to try to bring us down, He is there holding our hand and all we have to do is squeeze it and ask for help. My mom said something in our conversation that combined with the above passage to help put things back into perspective. She told me God wanted to use me in a big way. She explained my experiences could now be used to help people who have gone through what I have been through. She further explained there was a recovery program for men at our church, but not for women. She told me to think about it and look into it. I would have never thought in a million years what God wanted for the next steps of my journey.

I thought and prayed about it and even wrote in my journal about it, asking for God to guidance for what He wanted me to do. What was the purpose for this major event in my life? It was amazing how quickly He answered me. I wrote two journal entries and they are back to back. I asked one day and received the answer the next day.

May 6, 2012

A spiritual battle has been going on in me the last few days. My past addictions and discretions have been laying heavily on me. Doubt has risen to the surface and questions of my self-worth are forefront in my mind. As I am new in my faith I am learning to rely heavily on God and to put my full trust in Him. I am worthy! Although I may not deserve God's love I know that God loves me unconditionally.

Satan is attacking my new faith and trying to tear my faith apart. It will never work! I will rely and lean on my God and ask Him to strengthen me every minute, every second of every day. I may struggle but with God at my side, I know that Satan will never win.

My struggle is not knowing which direction God wants me to go. Where do you want me Lord and I will follow. Please show me the path you have planned for me. I know you have big plans for me Lord as Satan wouldn't be so eager to try and put distance between us. I thank you for being patient with me and softening my heart so I can now truly understand your love. I believe you will never leave my side, and for that alone I am eternally grateful.

May 7, 2012

God may have answered my prayers today. I got a call from church telling me they did not have a women's recovery group because they are looking for a leader. I may not be a mature enough Christian to lead the group just yet, but I told them I would be very interested in helping get a group started. There is such a strong need for it and since I need it maybe

God is showing me the path of where He wants me to be and serve Him. Since Satan has been attacking me with my own battles I know God is going to use it for good. If I have to struggle in order to help other people and lead them to Christ then I am willing to pay that price.

For the first time in my life I feel like I have a purpose and all I want to do is God's work and I'm so excited. I just pray that God will continue to work through myself and my church to get this group started. God is so awesome and amazing! He does answer prayers.

Indeed, God answers prayers. I went from having no clue as to what God wanted me to do, to going through a complete breakdown, and then seeing some clarity in the direction God wanted to take me. God rescued me twice. From those rescues came transformation to want to pay it forward and help others. I was rescued and being rescued inspires rescuing.

Chapter 7

Recovery

---------- ✳ ----------

*W*hen people hear the word "recovery," the words "drugs" and "alcohol" will most likely come to mind. However, recovery is not about a substance abuse problem, it is about recovering from a habitual sin problem. By using this term, we can start to see recovery can be more than substance abuse. It is about anything that enslaves us and separates us from God. True recovery is freedom in Christ and getting rid of the strongholds that keep us enslaved to sin. True freedom involves more than being sober in your habitual sin, but involves a heart transformation from knowing Jesus Christ.

Over time, society has largely accepted the characterization of addictions as diseases.

Therefore, many reading this book may be skeptical as to why habitual sin is being used to replace the word "addiction" in this book. Addiction may be a disease; however, that disease is our sin. It is not a disease in the sense that we catch or are born with alcoholism or drug addiction. People tend to use the word "disease" as a crutch for avoiding taking responsibility for their choices. It is a choice to pick up that drink and then the next one and then the next one. It is a choice to snort that line of cocaine or to choose to have that third serving of food as a mask to cover up emotions. So when we substitute the word "addiction" for habitual sin it takes away the excuses and the lack of responsibility in using the word "disease" and puts the responsibility of our own choices and our sin back on us.

What is sin? Sin can be considered anything we do that goes against God's commandments. Edward T. Welch, in his book *Addiction: A Banquent in the grave*, stated:Sin is ultimately against God. It is any failure to conform to the law of God in either action or attitude.

It is not only the actions that get us into trouble, but the mindset that we have going into those actions. For example, it is not a sin to drink alcohol; however, it is a sin to drink in excess. Anything in excess is considered a sin. So one may say, "I only had two glasses of wine." That is not in excess, but the mindset of those two glasses of wine was to drown the sorrows of that day, and instead of going to God for comfort and relief from those harsh emotions, this person went to alcohol. They went to get that immediate relief to take away their feelings. The mindset of why this person is drinking can be just as much a sin as drinking five glasses of wine just to have fun.

People often assume sin is always a person's conscious choice to disobey God; a person is always in complete control over saying yes or no to those choices. More often than not, addiction gives the appearance the substance is in control. An example of that can be found in something as simple as watching a commercial. A person with an alcohol addiction only has to see a vodka commercial on TV and find they are unable to resist getting up and getting that drink. It feels like the substance has taken control. I have been there too many times to count.

If you are or were like me, you would make the decision to not drink or do drugs. You would feel like you were in control and you put your foot down. You would be determined not to party that night. Then within thirty minutes of having made that decision, you would get invited to the bar. You would drag your feet a bit, but then decide to go. You convinced yourself it was okay to have a couple of drinks, but no drugs. You were at the bar with your third drink down and one of your friends decided to have an "after party" at their house. You were already a little tipsy by this point and your will power slowly caved in. You decide to go, but you resolve you are still not going to do drugs. You walk into the house and drugs are lined out on the coffee table. Before you know it, your resolve crumbles and it took no more than five minutes to do that first line. You know how it feels;

the second you saw it, your mouth started to salivate and your body went into overdrive craving the drugs. The cravings physically took over and your mind no longer had control. Before you knew it, the smart decision you thought you made a few hours prior came crashing in on you at full speed. You finally realize the drugs are in control, but are they?

How did you get to that point? Let's see, you stood in your living room one day and suddenly you craved drugs so bad, you had to start doing them? Is that right? Or, did you make choice after choice to pursue the alcohol and drugs until the substances controlled your body?

Edward T. Welch talks about this even further in his book:

> The disease model does not fit as well as we might think. The cravings and desires at the core of the addictive experience are not quite the same as an invading virus. If you catch a virus, you have no choice. You don't want it, and you would be glad to be rid of it. Heavy drinking, however, doesn't just happen to us. Instead, the drinker feels there are payoffs— however temporary—to drunkenness. (There are for any sin) In other words, addicts make choices to pursue their addiction.
>
> As one experienced drinker observed, "When the desire to drink hits me, I feel like I am

being pulled in different directions by two teams of horses."

"Which team wins?" asked a friend.

"Whichever one I say 'giddyap' to."

Even with all the associated misery, people drink because, on some level, drinking does something for them. Their drinking appears to be purposeful.

Coming to terms that addiction is habitual sin can be a new perspective for you. Maybe it is one that you are open to understanding, or maybe you are pushing it aside. There are differing viewpoints on the definition of addiction and whether or not it is a genetic disorder or disease. If it is a disease, how do you catch it? No matter which approach you take, the answer to freedom still remains the same: Jesus Christ. It is your choice whether or not you want to follow Him and truly receive the pure freedom that He longs to give you. Using other terms such as "addict" or "addiction" tends to point toward the perspective that the problem lies within the body and not the heart. Habitual sin is a heart issue and in order to repair the problem, you need a heart transformation only Jesus Christ can provide.

God gave us free will to make the choice to follow Him. It wouldn't mean anything if He forcefully compelled us to love Him. He wants us to freely choose Him so we can live a joyful and purposeful life.

The hardest part in starting your recovery and finding your freedom is realizing you have a problem and admitting the problem is not going to go away without some help. You cannot do it on your own. God used my neck surgery to get my attention and to show me there was work to be done. He shows each of us through our own unique understanding what it is we need to lay at Jesus' feet in order to receive true freedom from sin enslavement. In the process of accepting I had become dependent on the pain medication, a much bigger door of realization was opened. The magnitude of what God tried to show me was almost overwhelming. It tore across my soul like a hurricane hitting land and leaving a path of destruction so big I didn't even know how to begin healing.

Admitting there was a much bigger problem I needed to address was hard. I needed to contact my church and ask about a recovery program for women. Admission to struggling with any type of addiction is scary. The feelings of shame and embarrassment invade the mind and a battle of resistance begins to wage war internally. This ends up throwing the mind into a downward spiral. God wanted me to take that step to becoming free and Satan wanted me to feel worthless so I would not take those steps. I eventually grabbed my head and fell to my knees in tears not knowing what to do. I did not—no, I could not let Satan win as the only result would be to turn back to the one thing that is short-lived temporary pleasure.

God grants us these moments of clarity in the midst of our darkest chaos. Sometimes they are longer moments than others. These moments of clarity give us the ability to act upon our need to get help. So not only do we need to realize we have a problem that we can't fix ourselves, but we need to act upon that new found knowledge.

If you are a believer and already attend a church, the first step would be to reach out to your church. It can be as simple as reaching out to a friend who can help pray for you and work with you to understand your needs and identify the right program. Some churches already have recovery programs in place such as Celebrate Recovery or Setting Captives Free and would be a good starting point for getting plugged in. Bringing your sin and your struggles out of the darkness and into the light is a critical first step. Sin tends to hide in the darkness where no one can see what you are doing. This also means no one can help hold you accountable and be there to support you in your journey.

If you are not a believer in Jesus Christ, I pray Jesus opens your heart to make that choice to follow Him. As stated earlier, He is the only answer to your freedom. Jesus is the only one who can bring you to live in the light instead of wallowing in a sea of darkness where waves continuously crash down in an effort to drown you. Find a Christ-centered recovery program to attend on a regular basis; one that teaches scripture and digs deep into understanding the meaning of a relationship with Christ. Alcoholics Anonymous or Narcotics Anonymous is in just about every city. I recommend you go to these meetings immediately if the need is urgent. They are plentiful and more of those meetings are available at different time slots than you will find with a specific church-centered program. Regardless, as soon as possible, find a church to attend near you and get involved. Call the church office and share with them your struggles so they can help you. They will facilitate getting connected and help to find and identify available meetings to attend, especially if they do not already have a supporting program.

There is one important caveat, please know although Christ is the answer to finding your freedom from habitual sin, spiritual transformation and guidance cannot take place until you have safely gone through detoxification. There are several rehabilitation centers across the nation that can help you to break the physical dependence on substances. The ideal is if you can locate a Christ centered rehab center. Their ability and experience to help you through the detox stage in concert with spiritual support is important. Your mind will not be able to focus on God if it is solely focused on the physical withdrawals.

After contacting my church about a women's recovery group, they pointed me in the direction of a program called Setting Captives Free. As I shared with my church my former and current experiences, they immediately asked me to start in the program and connected me with a mentor. Setting Captives Free is a Bible-based program that centers your focus on God and teaches you who you are in Christ. It teaches when we choose anything other than Christ as our priority, it becomes a sin issue. It could be drinking excessively, drug abuse, overeating, money, careers, and many more things. I had a lot to learn. Every time we choose to drink until we can't see straight, or we go straight to a whole pint of ice cream, we are choosing to go to things of this world instead of leaning on Christ. It taught me the meaning of living water and how Jesus is that living water and He is the only one who can quench our thirst.

There may have been many injustices that could have completely brought you to rock bottom. Maybe it was sexual and/or physical abuse growing up or even in a relationship as an adult. Maybe it was losing someone so dear to your heart that the physical ache was overwhelming. These kinds of circumstances can crush you and completely break you. All you feel is pain and agony. The memories swarm in from every angle. It is hard not to want immediate relief from the pain and anguish even if it is only temporary. However, we need to understand and believe healing comes by fighting through the pain, leaning on Christ, and asking Him to give us the strength to get through the trials happening to us. It's not fair that bad things happen to good people, but we live in an imperfect, fallen world; a world full of sin. All we can do is fall on our knees and ask God to relieve us of the pain and have hope that beyond this life, there will be a time where there will be no more pain and suffering. There will be no more tears. I know—easier said than done. This life is hard with its constant struggles. However, if we could learn the truths and the tools to use to get through life the right way, then we can start to feel the peace, love, and joy of clutching to Christ's hand while He leads the way.

So do not fear, for I am with you; do not be dismayed, for I am your God. I will strengthen you and help you; I will uphold you with my righteous right hand. All who rage against you will surely be ashamed and disgraced; those who oppose you will be as nothing and perish. Though you search for your enemies, you will not find them. Those who wage war against you will be as nothing at all. For I am the Lord your God who takes hold of your right hand and says to you, "Do not fear; I will help you." —Isaiah 41:10-13

Some of you are reading this and rolling skeptical eyes. You are thinking I don't know you or understand your experience. Or maybe you are hearing something similar in church and wondering the same thing. I used to think this way, and to be honest, there are a lot of people who will try and give you advice who do not have an understanding of your experience. They will sincerely, but self-righteously tell you that Jesus can be your rock and you will get through it. They will tell you that they will pray for you, but again in a self-righteous way. Often, these types of Christians do not follow up with actions. Don't get me wrong—people praying for you is one of the most important elements of recovery, but when presented in the wrong context, it is not what you want or need to hear. You may want to tell them to shut up. You sense more judgment from these Christians rather than understanding love. It does not help that your mindset may be defensive because you are not ready to let go of that bottle or other dependency of comfort.

I have felt all of these emotions, especially before I surrendered to Christ. My family would point me to Christ and get on me about going to church. They couldn't understand why I would make the choices I did, and why I couldn't open my life to Christ and start being good. Keep in mind these were the feelings I felt and not necessarily my family's intentions. Nonetheless, it pushed me away because I felt they couldn't understand me. I finally came to the place where I understood not everyone would understand, but if people tried to point me to Christ and tried to give me advice on how to get through situations, it was because they loved me. Yes, some of the people I encountered were judgmental and self-righteous and I had to learn they are people too. As much as I may not have agreed with them, it was their sin to which they would need to answer and not my own.

One day, my brother preached God's Word to a couple thousand high school students. I was lucky enough to see him teach these kids. He told a story I had heard before, but from a perspective that hit home. To this day, I still look at that moment of epiphany and wish I had realized it years earlier during my hard times. It was the story of the woman who suffered from bleeding for twelve years and touched Jesus' robe for healing.

In this story, a man ran over to Jesus asking Him to heal his sick daughter who was twelve years of age; as Jesus walked, He had His disciples with Him and a crowd of people had been following Him, wanting to see Him perform miracles and to hear Him preach. People began to crowd Him and the disciples as they continued to walk. Picture this with me: you are at a concert and you are front and center of the stage, right down in the mosh pit. If you have ever been down in that section of a concert, it is pure craziness. People are pushing left and right; you start to sweat because you have a thousand people squished into a small area designated for far fewer people. You have no idea who is next to you or in front of you, and you definitely don't know who is behind you. There are too many people pushing to get closer to the stage, trying to hear the music and get close to the band. This is what I picture when reading this story. It may have not been exactly like that, but there was a big crowd trying to get close to Jesus.

As Jesus is walking to this man's house to see his daughter, a woman comes up behind Jesus and touches the bottom of His cloak. This woman had bled for twelve years and no one could heal her. Back in that day when you had a health issue or a disease, you were labeled unclean and outcast from normal society. So as you can imagine, she snuck up in the middle of the crowd and crouched low, probably crawling on her knees to touch His cloak. She didn't want anyone to see her or know she was there, as she knew she would be mocked and chastised by the people. However, somehow she had enough faith and belief in Jesus that she believed if she could touch His cloak, she would be healed, and she was. As soon as she touched the cloak, her bleeding stopped.

Jesus stopped immediately and asked, "Who touched my cloak?" Now the crowd pressed in and crushed Jesus and the disciples. So many people are bumping and pushing, it was no surprise when Peter gently pointed out everyone pushed up against Jesus and many most likely touched His cloak. Peter did not think twice about it, but Jesus knew what happened.

But Jesus said, "Someone touched me; I know that power has gone out from me." Then the woman, seeing that she could not go unnoticed, came trembling and fell at his feet. In the presence of all the people, she told why she had touched him and how she had been instantly healed. Then he said to her, "Daughter, your faith has healed you. Go in peace." —Luke 8:46-48

Keep in mind: this woman was an outcast from society. The last thing she wanted was to be in the spotlight. However, her faith overcame her fear. She believed Jesus could heal her and it was that faith that healed her. Although faith was one of the main points of the story, it is important to point out something else. In the midst of the overwhelming, crushing crowd, Jesus knew the woman had touched His cloak. No one else saw or understood the woman's years-long experience with her affliction. In fact, the people had more than likely cast her out to die with everyone else who was considered to be unclean. They did not understand her circumstances, but Jesus knew. He knew her experience and the state of her heart the moment she touched his cloak. He knew the level of her faith and she was at rock bottom. She chose to believe in Jesus and to follow Him, knowing He could indeed heal her.

Perhaps you are in the beginning stages of your recovery process or maybe you have already gone through it, but remember, a lot of people will not understand your situation or experience, but Jesus knows. He knows everything you have gone through, done, and what has been done to you. He understands and He still loves you. He wants to get to know you or get reacquainted with you. So don't let the perception of "no one understands" impede your recovery process. Jesus will be right there waiting for you to lean on Him and He will provide someone as His messenger that does understand and can relate to what you are going through.

Chapter 8

Guilty Shame

———— ❋ ————

"Do not be afraid; you will not be put to shame. Do not fear disgrace; you will not be humiliated. You will forget the shame of your youth and remember no more the reproach of your widowhood." —
Isaiah 54:4 (NIV)

*S*atan's number one tactic for bringing us down is to highlight and exploit feelings of guilt and shame. These feelings are often recognized as a knot in your stomach that shoots through your heart when you realize all of the things you have done. The knot originates as thoughts like ripples in the ocean and builds until eventually they end up as fifteen foot waves crashing down on you. Often, you are in denial about the building waves until they thrash your body into a tumbling mess. You try to get to the surface of the water so you can get a breath of fresh air, but you soon don't know which way is up. Your lungs start to burn and panic sets in. You start to feel like you may not live to see another day. Satan's goal is to keep you tumbling in the water so you can't surface to catch your breath. He doesn't want you to gain control and come back to knowing who you are in Christ.

Shame can hinder you from finding that freedom in Christ and realizing your value is in Him and not in the things of your past. For too long, I allowed shame to keep me from living out God's will for me. Feelings of worthlessness would creep into the small crevices of my mind and attach themselves to my core. Eventually the personality I presented became a front for all of my insecurities. I exaggerated my confidence to those around me so no one would know I felt worthless inside, even further confusing my identity.

Rejection was one of my biggest fears. I experienced it in a number of ways: men who told me that I wasn't worth more than a "good night," good "friends" themselves feeling rejection, turned on me after I left Florida by sending the message I was no longer worth their time. It was manifested in the fear that in my new life, people would find out everything I had done, or they would discover my flaws and cast doubt as to whether I could add value to a friendship. I pictured it in my head; the judgment of people finding out I had done drugs and coming to the conclusion I was tainted goods. The judging of my sexual promiscuity and I could no longer be "pure." However, in my darkness, I was determined for that not to happen to me and as a result, I pushed people away. I went from one extreme of going from relationship to relationship to avoiding even the option to be in a relationship. The fear of rejection paralyzed and prevented me from being able to love and be loved.

It wasn't about finding a husband; it was about completely shutting down the ability to be able to love in the capacity that God calls us to love. I didn't love my friends or my family in accordance with God's commandments. We must set aside our fear of rejection and have faith in God. We may go through struggles in life, but we can't live life through a prism of fear, constantly seeking our heart's desire through a distorted lens of reality. Fear of rejection will stop us in our tracks from ever reaching those desires. This is not what God wants from us or for us.

God wants us to step off that cliff in faith knowing He will catch us. The only way to overcome the shame and guilt we feel for our sins is to acknowledge God is the only one who matters in our judgment. If we accept Jesus as our Lord and Savior, we are covered by His death on the cross. He is our redemption, our redeeming love. We are forgiven for our sins—past, present, and future.

My greatest challenge was continuing to ask for God's forgiveness every time I experienced feelings of despair and shame. This is another tool of Satan; to cause us to doubt our forgiveness in Christ. To make us think God could not possibly forgive us once and for all. However, continuing to ask for forgiveness from God multiple times causes Him pain and sorrow in the demonstration of our unbelief. We are, in our hearts and minds, invalidating His death on the cross by not accepting His promise of complete and final forgiveness. Our sins are washed clean as snow. There is no more blood to be spilled on those sins. The problem lies in whether or not we are willing to forgive ourselves.

Forgiving ourselves is the key to unlocking the door to God's blessings and plans for us. It is a part of the healing process. If we are not able to forgive ourselves, then a darkness starts to brew in our hearts and leads the way to falling back into Satan's grasp. We can be our own worst enemy. The temptations start to get stronger and left unchecked, will ultimately drown our emotions in something other than Christ. We need to be able to arrest our shameful thoughts and lay them at Jesus' feet. If God can love us enough to forgive our sins, we need to be able to let go of our shame and move forward. God will use everything for good. Peter is a classic example.

Peter loved Jesus with all his heart and promised to follow Jesus into eternity. Even after Jesus told him He would deny him three times, Peter refused to believe it. In his mind, there was no way he would deny the Son of God, especially after everything he had witnessed. Yet, later that night, as Jesus was arrested and brought in for trial, Peter did just that.

In the chaos and commotion, the crowd asked Peter if Jesus was the man he had followed. Peter immediately denied it. Fear gripped him and he was unable to boldly say He was a follower of Jesus.

Peter's reaction to his fear revealed his own shameful state. Put yourself in Peter's sandals and imagine being a disciple of Jesus for three years. You have been in His presence day and night, learning from Him, and realizing the love you have for Him and knowing He is truth. Peter gave up His career as a fisherman to follow Jesus and to become a fisher of men. That takes a leap of faith and some serious trust. Yet Peter, when it came down to it, denied Jesus not once, not twice, but three times. I don't know about you, but the shame and guilt that would come pouring over me would be overwhelming. I think I would crawl up in a ball in a dark room never to show my face again. How could I face anyone especially Jesus when I had failed so miserably.

Yet Peter did not shut down or disappear. He continued, after Jesus' death, to disciple others and showed them the righteous path to follow. This tells us that he not only sought Jesus' forgiveness, but he forgave himself as well, which allowed him to live out God's will. We must not let our shame hinder us to the point of disobedience. Not only will we deny ourselves the blessings that God wants to give us, but also we deny the people God wants us to help.

To give up shame means to look to Jesus. Our thoughts should be focused on Him and His redemption. God has redeemed us by His sacrificial actions and love. When we choose Jesus Christ, we are no longer slaves to our emotions and our thoughts. Knowing God, even in our brokenness, sees the goodness in us creates an amazing sense of freedom. It took me a long time to come to this realization. For the first few years, Satan held me captive in my thoughts of shame and guilt. It wouldn't take much to trigger flashbacks of my Florida days or even before then when I was in San Diego; something as small as a song on the radio would send me into a state of insecurity. These flashback memories of past shameful sins would start to play in my mind over and over again, which would then trigger another set of memories. One of the memories Satan always tried to use was my drug use after I returned from Florida. He tried to use this to bring me down and make me feel that I couldn't run from the drugs, it was hard coded in my DNA, and there was no way out so I might as well give in to the temptations of pure bliss forever.

I came home from Florida thinking I pulled myself away from the drugs and the bad crowd. It was a good decision, but it was only the beginning. My habits and my way of thinking needed to change as well. I no longer had the same access to drugs and that helped as long as I did not have a connection. Well, that did not last long as I soon found a connection again. I dated someone who had a friend who had access to cocaine. We were out partying one night and there it was, spread out on the kitchen counter. It was a big flashing beacon of temptation. The thoughts that went through my head were unfortunately pure excitement. I couldn't wait to do it again. Somehow I forgot the destructive path I left behind in Florida and the only thing my mind focused on was the feeling I would have after snorting that first line. The high my body would feel was the only focus of my thoughts. The decision was already made. I wasn't following Christ at this time, so I had no armor to put on me. I had no action plan for me to run away, and of course my boyfriend at the time decided he would partake even though it wasn't a normal occurrence for him. It seemed the deck was stacked, so why not, right? That was the start of another downward spiral, but this time I knew better. The conviction and shame came a lot quicker this time, but still didn't stop me until one event shook me enough, it stopped me in my tracks. We were partying one night and I had made the commitment to meet my mom at an exercise boot camp early the next morning. However, my desire to snort lines of coke was more important to me. I remember telling myself multiple times this is the last line because I have to get up early in the morning. I couldn't say no every time another round was prepared. I eventually went to bed, but I only got a couple hours of sleep before my alarm went off. My body was a wreck. I had a headache the size of Texas and there was no way I would make the boot camp. Having to make that phone call to cancel on my mom was a wake-up call. Disappointing my mom was the last thing I wanted to do. I couldn't tell her that I had stayed up all night doing drugs, but oddly enough, I felt I could tell her that I had too much drink. That felt like a little bit more of an acceptable lie even though the point is I canceled on her regardless of the reason. When we are addicted to certain behaviors, it is interesting how we rationalize one as being more acceptable than others.

My relationship with my parents was better and the last thing I wanted to do was destroy it again. God's conviction quickly turned into condemnation. I felt sick to my stomach that whole day. Not only did my body go through a physical hangover, but my soul went through a hangover of its own. The drugs began to undermine my efforts to repair my relationships. The shame and guilt I felt lasted a long time and brought my insecurities back into play. This bout of drug use didn't last long, praise the Lord, but it still did damage to my soul.

Satan tried to bring me down again using my sense of shame to lower my self-worth and make me feel I wasn't good enough for anyone. I have to admit he succeeded for quite some time. In the long run, we can claim Jesus Christ as our Lord and Savior and claim victory over our lives through Him. No longer will Satan be able to win the war. Are you ready to claim victory over your emotions of shame and guilt? Are you ready to climb out of the muddy hole and into God's loving arms? No longer do we need to be slaves to our emotions. We must consistently lay them at Jesus' feet. We must forgive ourselves as Jesus forgave us so we can walk forward into the light of victory.

"It is for freedom that Christ has set us free. Stand firm, then, and do not let yourselves be burdened again by a yoke of slavery." —Galatians 5:1 (NIV)

Conviction comes from God, but condemnation comes from Satan. God will convict our hearts when He feels we have sinful behavior that could separate us from Him. It is that feeling of wanting to lay out our sins and ask for forgiveness. There are times though when Satan will capitalize on that conviction and exploit our vulnerabilities to highlight our shame and condemnation. It is a thin line between accepting we are no longer being convicted for our actions and continuing to beat ourselves up by basking in the gloom and guilt of our past actions. This is prime ground for Satan to bring us down. Realizing where the line is drawn helps us to overcome those thoughts before they do too much damage.

Jesus illustrates this line in the story of a woman who was brought before him and accused of adultery. As she was paraded in front of the crowd by a group of Pharisees, I could only imagine the amount of shame and fear she must have felt. As she was ready to be convicted of her crimes, Jesus stepped in and began to write with His finger in the sand.

At dawn he appeared again in the temple courts; where all the people gathered around him, and he sat down to teach them. The teachers of the law and the Pharisees brought in a woman caught in adultery. They made her stand before the group and said to Jesus, "Teacher, this woman was caught in the act of adultery. In the Law Moses commanded us to stone such women. Now what do you say?" They were using this question as a trap, in order to have a basis for accusing him.

But Jesus bent down and started to write on the ground with his finger. When they kept on questioning him, he straightened up and said to them, "Let any one of you who is without sin be the first to throw a stone at her." Again he stooped down and wrote on the ground.

At this, those who heard began to go away one at a time, the older ones first, until only Jesus was left, with the woman still standing there. Jesus straightened up and asked her, "Woman, where are they? Has no one condemned you?"

"No one, sir" she said.

"Then neither do I condemn you," Jesus declared. "Go now and leave your life of sin."

—Luke 8 1-11 (NIV)

Shame crouches around corners and lurks in the darkness to grab you at every opportunity.

"Be alert and of sober mind, your enemy the devil prowls around like a roaring lion looking for someone to devour. Resist him, standing firm in the faith, because you know that the family of believers throughout the world is undergoing the same kind of sufferings." — 1 Peter 5:8-9

In the darkness of our sin, shame is internal, yet the moment we get exposed, the shame magnifies itself ten times over. Your face starts to flush and the temperature increases instantly. Your heart feels like it is going to pound out of your chest and you want to crawl into a hole where you can't ever be seen. I could only imagine this is what this woman felt as she was pulled in front of a crowd of strangers and humiliated as someone who broke the law and is not worthy.

I have no idea what Jesus wrote in the sand since it wasn't stated, but the story was powerful in turning the tables on the Pharisees and showing the sin within their own lives. Jesus does not condemn and He tells us not to judge one another. It is not our burden to carry. We should not be condemning others for their sins when we have our own sin to worry about. If you are like me, a lot of my guilt, shame, and embarrassment came from my own internally self-condemning thoughts, but in reality, Jesus is the only one who can judge us on the Day of Judgment. We place this extra burden of people's thoughts and opinions on our shoulders when there is no need for it. Jesus doesn't shame us, nor does He use guilt to force us into doing things. Jesus is about providing love and forgiveness and the ultimate gift of grace. Jesus is the only one we should focus on for our approval and our value. When feelings of shame send us into that downward spiral, we need to call out to the Lord. Put Him as our focus and use it as a shield to help protect against those negative emotions that separate us from the blessing of a relationship with Christ.

Just like the woman caught in adultery, Jesus forgave our sins and told us to go and sin no more. We need to have faith God will use our sinful past for good. I have finally gotten to the point where I thank God every day for allowing me to go through everything I have because had I not, I wouldn't be able to help other women tear through that veil of darkness and see the light of hope. You may be in the beginning stages of healing, or you have long since found your freedom, but wherever you are in your struggles, God has a purpose and a divine plan for you. Our experiences allow us to see the brokenness in other people more clearly and understand the struggles that they are going through. Jesus has allowed us to go through our own circumstances so we may be that messenger for someone else. We understand the pain. We understand the surrender that is needed. We understand the struggles. We understand the shame, and we can or will understand that light of freedom that comes after that exhausting climb out of the pit.

We need to continue to keep our eyes open and attuned to thoughts full of shame and condemnation. We need to arrest those thoughts and lay them at Jesus' feet every single time. That is how we become free from the guilt and shame Satan tries to conjure up in our hearts. Knowing who we are in Christ diminishes the lack of security in who we believe we are.

"Therefore, there is now no condemnation for those who are in Christ Jesus". —Romans 8:1 (NIV)

Chapter 9

True Love

——— ✳ ———

ove. Love was the one thing I so desperately sought. My mind reeled with the thought of how I could have gotten it so wrong? I had been looking for a man to fill that void in my heart, thinking if I could find someone who would love me unconditionally, then I would be perfectly happy. That person would accept me as I am. My priority was to find someone I could come home to and talk about my day. So when there was a bad day, he would wrap his arms around me, comfort me, and tell me everything would be all right. I needed that security of knowing I was valued. It gave me purpose. I wanted to mean something in this world. If I had a husband and a family, then I felt that would give me the value I desperately needed. There is a misconception that happiness is to be sought and found within the walls of this world and amongst men. A man was on my pedestal, and a man was my God.

It wasn't until I was rescued and built a relationship with Jesus that I finally realized I had a false sense of the meaning of love. I had searched for something to fill that void and I had tried everything within this world to overcome the loneliness I felt, only to learn that the answer was not of this world. It was found in Jesus Christ. God is love. He embodies it and gives it unconditionally to His children. True love was found within God and is God. Love is God's very essence.

Romans 12:9-21 says:

Love must be sincere. Hate what is evil; cling to what is good. Be devoted to one another in love. Honor one another above yourselves. Never be lacking in zeal, but keep your spiritual fervor, serving the Lord. Be joyful in hope, patient in affliction, and faithful in prayer. Share with the Lord's people who are in need. Practice hospitality. Bless those who persecute you; bless and do not curse. Rejoice with those who rejoice; mourn with those who mourn. Live in harmony with one another. Do not be proud, but be willing to associate with people of low position. Do not be conceited. Do not repay anyone evil for evil. Be careful to do what is right in the eyes of everyone. If it is possible, as far as it depends on you, live at peace with everyone. Do not take revenge, my dear friends, but leave room for God's wrath, for it is written: "It is mine to avenge; I will repay," says the Lord. On the contrary: "If your enemy is hungry, feed him; if he is thirsty, give him something to drink. In doing this, you will heap burning coals on his head." Do not be overcome by evil, but overcome evil with good.

By this definition, it was clear I had no clue about love and what it meant. It was all about me and what someone could provide me. When I met someone, I would ask myself, *does this someone give me that butterfly feeling and make my heart go pitter-patter?* If they didn't, there was no interest. It was a constant feeling of joy and happiness for which I searched. I think we all know a constant state of happiness is far from possible, yet we continue to chase it like a lost red scarf blowing in the wind.

As I thought about this, I heard a message at church on sincere love. God spoke to me through that sermon. The pastor talked about the four myths of love and what the biblical answers are to those myths.

Myth #1: Love is *just* a feeling.

The tendency of this world is to believe love comes naturally. When people get divorced or separated, I hear a lot of people say, "people fall in and out of love all the time." In reality, love is a choice we have to make every day. We need to ask ourselves, are we *choosing* to love those around us? Love is hard and can be difficult, but it is about making a choice to love through those hard times and to work at our relationships. Imagine if God got upset with us, like we do with others, for the way we live our lives or the decisions we make? Like us, He may well lose His feeling of love for us and then what? Can you imagine God deciding not to love us because He "fell out of love" over our choice to sin? No, of course not; that would completely invalidate the whole purpose of the gospel. God chooses to love us unconditionally. He chooses to bless us when we are obedient and to shower His peace and comfort into our souls through the Holy Spirit. When we are feeling down, He is there to lift us up. When we are completely broken, He is there to say, "I will show you the way." He does all those things because He *chooses* to love us. For us, love is like a roller coaster; it is sometimes a hard, slow climb up the hill. You can almost hear the *click, click, click* of the chain pulling you to the top. But when you get to the top and come over the crest, the drop is absolutely thrilling. Our hands all of a sudden come up in the air and as the wind whips into our faces, we are smiling and giggling uncontrollably. There is nothing like it. Then we know all of the hard work of loving is well worth the effort.

Constantly chasing this feeling of butterfly-love was the goal in my life. Has it been like this in your life? Do you feel that way now? Have you chased the impossible feeling of constant happiness only to be sorely disappointed? Each time we are disappointed it feels like plunging down a steep cliff and feeling every scrape and bruise, maybe even some broken bones. We get to the bottom and look up with teary eyes at what feels to be an impossible climb back to the top. We become gun-shy at taking another chance only to be hurt again. Our confidence and self-esteem take another hit. Some of us might give up for a while; and some of us, stubborn and hard headed, start that climb again, only to fall over and over again.

How do we get past the point of disappointment and giving up and trying to move on to the next thing? We understand God is love and it is His purpose for us to choose to love each other. We may even have the head knowledge of how tough it is to love like that. However, the knowledge that it is a choice escapes a lot of us when the world we live in bombards us with messages that encourage self-centeredness to do whatever makes us happy. There will be times of disappointment, but our success to work through it will increase significantly if we realize it is a choice within our control. Love is not *just* a feeling, it is a sacrificial choice and the result of that choice is pure joy, but only with God. Directing our love to God instead of man is our only hope to satisfy the needs of our human souls.

Myth #2: Love just happens. We cannot help it; we have no control over it. We cannot help who we fall in love with.

For a long time, I had this same misconception; I would know it when I saw it, right? My thought process through the years has always been love happens. People talk about love at first sight, but is that true? If we are not consistently choosing to love through the roller coaster of our feelings, then how can we be in love? Maybe, just maybe, we have fallen in and out of <u>lust</u> instead of love. I know I have. This definition of love blew my mind and changed my whole perspective on the true meaning of love. We need to understand the biblical meaning of true love in order to fully benefit from the blessings of God's love.

There is a story in the bible of Amnon and Tamar. They were half-brother and half-sister and Amnon was King David's son. Over time, Amnon fell in love with Tamar to the point he became obsessed and felt that he had to have her, so he devised a plan of trickery. He pretended to be sick and asked for Tamar to come in and comfort him. He forcefully had his way with her even after she pleaded with him to think about what he was doing. Afterward, he was full of rage and hatred over what had transpired with Tamar. Amnon was not in love with Tamar; he was in lust. He did not understand the concept of true love. Amnon had a sense of entitlement that he should be able to fulfill his desires no matter the cost to anyone else. He demanded he not go a second without filling his needs and desires because of his position within the kingdom.

How often do we have the overwhelming compulsion to do whatever it takes to get what our heart desires? Have you ever felt something for someone and then either throw yourself way out there to get their attention, or devise a plan to gradually gain their attention by adjusting your personality to fit theirs? If you are successful, then before he or she knows it, you have conquered your quest of fulfilling your own desires. We may not devise a plan such as Amnon's, but there is a parallel in his story. It is basic human nature to be selfish and self-centered and to have and cater to that feeling we deserve happiness in this world and we are entitled to it at all costs.

I cannot begin to tell you how many times I did things to fit in with the group of the guy that I wanted to be with. Adjusting who we are is not the answer to fulfilling our happiness, because when you look at it, love does not just happen. There is a part of us that will make unnecessary adjustments because we think the person over in this group will make us happy, and when they don't, we jump into another group. We adjust our personalities to match what we think they want and then onto the next group, until one day we wake up and realize we have no idea who we are. What do we truly want in our lives? What makes us happy and brings us joy beyond the men we put up on pedestals? By the time I left Florida, my name was just a name. I no longer had an identity that was associated with my birth name of Courtney. Love was not happening for me and I couldn't figure out why.

Ultimately, I realized the answer: God's love is consistent and unconditional. I still can't fathom that thought. It makes me speechless to think even after all of the things I have done or said or still decide to do, the things that separate me from God, He still continues to choose to love me. I don't think I will ever be able to fully comprehend that knowledge until I am in heaven. Think about that for a moment. If God chooses to love me unconditionally after all of the drugs I have done, after the sexual promiscuity, after repeatedly seeing my deceitful heart, after my acute self-centeredness that allowed me to walk over anyone to get what I wanted, then I have no other choice but to believe I have found love and I am loved. The good news is His love extends to and is available to everyone, including you, dear reader. You are loved. You may not understand this concept or maybe you do, but you are loved unconditionally. Tears roll down my smiling face thinking about the grace God has given me; the grace that is built from His foundation of love. So if God can continue to love me even after my past, and for whatever I might do in the future, He can love you too, no matter what your circumstances. You have to open your heart and believe.

Myth #3: Love is about getting what we want. It is all about feelings.

We are selfish in nature, so instinctively I think we view love as pleasing ourselves. Isn't it about how it makes us feel? When you ask someone why they love someone, isn't the typical response something like "well they make me feel good, they love me, they value me, they are beautiful"? It's all about how they make us feel, but love should be done more outwardly and it needs to be in more of a sacrificial manner.

"But I tell you, love your enemies and pray for those who persecute you." —Matthew 5:44

"For God so loved the world that He gave His only begotten Son." —John 3:16

Throughout the Bible, God tells us love is supposed to be sacrificial. It is critical to look into our own lives and determine whether we are putting conditions on our love or whether we are being purely sacrificial with our love.

This myth ties in with all of the other myths when it comes to thinking love is all about us and our self-centered needs; in how we focus on how it makes us feel, on getting what we want and what others can provide for us. When I told you the story about my friend and the loss of her brother, I demonstrated we can live our lives in a way that prioritizes our needs and not the needs of others. This is the complete opposite of what God teaches in His Word.

His number one commandment is to love Him and our neighbor. Love is what He wants us to pour out into this world. Love is making sure the other person gets a glimpse of God's glory, not of what we want or desire. It is not about us. Imagine a world where others thought more of others and living God's way of truth and love than living to please themselves. What a world that would be!

Myth #4: If we love, than love is accepting of everything.

This is a big one. Are we called to be tolerant in everything anyone does because we need to sacrificially love? The answer is no. Many people equate tolerance and unconditional love with acceptance and approval. However, it is important to remember God's love is based in truth and nothing else. It is possible to unconditionally love someone while not agreeing with their choices in how they live. We should not respond in a negative, judgmental way. Instead, we have a responsibility to gently "call out" our brothers and sisters in Christ to let them know because we love them, we need to tell them what they are doing is wrong. This is often difficult, but if God's love is based on His truth, then we must be obedient as it demonstrates our understanding of the difference between sincere, unconditional love and the perceived acceptance of sinful behaviors. We cannot refrain from the admonishment simply because they may not like us anymore. Again, because it is not about us, it is about them. Likewise, if we are on the receiving side of admonishment, we need to avoid being defensive and look into the sincerity of their words, as well as our own hearts for any truth to the matter.

One of the side results of being rescued by God is a new desire to help others. It took me a long time to figure out everything I tried to bring to my life is found in God. So when I did find it, I wanted nothing more than to spread the good news. I eventually ended up helping lead a women's recovery group for my church. It is a hard, dark ministry, especially when so many of the women are deep in darkness and only get occasional slivers of light from God. Even then it feels impossible for them to grasp.

There was one lady who had started coming to our group. She struggled with crack and drinking for over fifteen years with occasional spurts of sobriety, only to once again fall deep into the abyss of darkness that has a stronghold on her life. Even worse, she thought she deserved it. Her self-esteem was non-existent. My heart broke for her because I had once been there; not to the same depth of darkness, but most certainly I identified with the feelings worthlessness and being undeserving of God's grace and love. She also struggles with homosexuality and hates herself for being attracted to women, but at the same time doesn't understand why she can't get rid of the compulsion to pursue this attraction. She intellectually understands that she is a child of God yet she struggles with fully surrendering to Him. She has moments of sobriety and resolve where she is on fire for God and her real identity comes through. However, the demons are too strong for her to fight on her own and without full surrender, she eventually falls and stumbles back into darkness.

I love this woman dearly and she has a special place in my heart, but loving her means I can't accept her lifestyle of sin and I have a responsibility as a child of God and as her mentor to lovingly tell her in truth that her lifestyle is full of sin. Continuously turning her to Christ is my responsibility, but the rest is up to her and God. What a fine line that is for someone who wants to love unconditionally, but knows love means to love the person, but draw the boundaries in not overlooking the sin.

Sometimes, the only thing love requires is prayer and pointing back to God's truth when people reach out. Setting boundaries is hard, but comes with the answer to the myth. Love does not require condoning different people's opinions and being tolerant if it goes against God's word. We can love that person by giving them tough love. The one thing I am learning in leading a recovery group is realizing what I put my parents through all those years. They knew what it meant to love according to God's Word. They prayed for me, but stuck to their guns in making me pull myself out of the hole that I put myself in. Tough love requires God's strength and being able to take a step back and say there is nothing I can do for you, as that would enable you to continue in your behaviors. Instead, pray and let you know I am here for you when you decide to walk in the light once again. Until that time, you are on your own.

Love requires faith and truth. Without faith and believing God is love, there is no real understanding of what true love can provide. God can provide that stability of peace and joy that we so long for, but that only comes with believing God is love. He embodies love. He embraces love, and He promises love. Once I opened my eyes to this fact and understood, my world was turned upside down and I had my true "a-ha" moment.

So after everything I have done, I know God's love is the answer for my future and it is the answer for your future as well. We need to get away from the notion of what love is in today's world and substitute it for the biblical definition that states love equals a choice to commit to consistent sacrificial actions based on the truth of God's Word. Once we can do that, we are on the way to full recovery in our freedom through Jesus Christ.

Chapter 10

Who Am I?

——— ✳ ———

"When I embrace the truth that the foundation of my identity is the fact that I have been created in the image of God, it gives my life great dignity, value, security, significance, and purpose."
Pastor Kent Sparks, Beachcities
Community Church

Thoughts danced around in my mind when I woke up in the morning and knew I had scheduled four hours to write that day. I planned to write about who we are in Christ and the identity we should build in Jesus. I outlined what I wanted to say as I straightened my hair for church that morning. I walked into church and looked down at the sermon outline and saw it was titled, "Do you know who you are?" My eyes moistened, as I knew God had laid this issue on my heart to share; this was confirmation of the importance of this topic. It is one of the most important concepts to understand in order to have a fulfilling relationship with Christ. We cannot become free from our enslavement to sin if we do not know our true identity.

If I were to ask you, "Who are you?" What would be your response? It may be a simple question, but it becomes more difficult when you know the meaning and the power behind the question. Most of you would start to answer with something like, "well, I'm a mother of two," or, "I am an accountant." You might tell where you live and maybe even tell about your hobbies; is that you? Is your identity wrapped up in your career or your family? Do you rely solely on who you are in the world based on your functional purpose? If you were to lose your job or career, would you lose yourself in the midst of not knowing what you would do next? If you were to lose your family or your friends, would you experience an identity crisis? If you strip away the possibility of answering the question with a functional purpose, then how would you answer?

The answer should be based in what we want to emulate in this world. For me, my identity is in Christ. I am someone who is far from perfect, but who strives to live a life that glorifies Christ's name. As a believer in Christ, your identity should be in your Heavenly Father since you were created in His image. Your value becomes intrinsic as opposed to functional when you truly lay your life down to

follow Christ. Too often society is used as a barom-
eter to gauge what is viewed as significant and to get
confirmation of identity; for example, a good-paying
job or career as defined by others. Are you married?
Do you have kids? The perception of our culture
today relies on materialistic aspects of our world
and the confirmation of others saying well done. I,
like so many others, succumbed to this pressure and
found myself trapped in this satanic web of identity
deception.

For far too long I found my identity to be in the
midst of whether or not I had a man, family, and
friends. More importantly I thought my value was in
what other people thought of me. I felt I had no value
if it was only me. My identity was wrapped up in my
social status. I believed a large group of friends was
a measure of popularity and therefore meant I was
wanted and accepted and it spoke directly to my self-
worth. Most of these feelings and emotions stemmed
from my childhood and not understanding the true
meaning of love. This partly derived from experiences where I was called names and ostracized from
the groups from which I craved acceptance. Yet, all it
did was increase my heart's desire for it. Magnifying
the acceptance within a social circle was what I
wanted to aim for in life. That was my ultimate goal.
I dreamed of having an unlimited number of friends.
I remember even telling someone that I had enough
friends to choose a new friend each day to hang out
with and not run out for a year. I was full of pride,

as I had finally conquered my goal. The perception I had of myself was I was a girl everyone wanted to party with. No longer would I be the outcast. No longer would I be picked on and shamed. What a broken mess my heart was in.

Self-perception determines your identity and your self-direction. My pastor once said some profound words that sunk deep down into my soul. How we view ourselves can be good and can also be damaging, but most importantly, it determines how we are going to live our lives. My self-perception was full of insecurities and so I was driven to act in ways that would bring a level of acceptance that would replace my bucket of self-doubts with a bucket of inspiring admiration. My goal was to be a chameleon and blend in with whatever group I thought would pay attention to me. The problem with that is I would change my appearance and behavior to whatever they perceived to be cool and accepted.

In today's culture, it is not unusual for a woman's identity to be wrapped up in their sexuality. The media plays a large part in that, between pushing women to be a model size zero, to promoting the wearing of skimpy bikinis at the beach. The image is portrayed that a woman's value is increased when you have that nice body, you dress sexy, and you look young and flawless. It is no longer accepted to be who you are. The saying, "as long as you are beautiful on the inside, then nothing else matters," doesn't appear to be demonstrated in reality. It is worse today than ever before and I fell into that trap. My level of acceptance needed to be fed and that meant I followed the crowd in wearing the sexy clothing with the short shorts and the low cut shirts. Carl's Jr. Restaurant commercials portray this concept to a "T" by using scantily clad models eating hamburgers and using their sex appeal to lure in the business. Sex sells right? Over time, this behavior desensitizes people and begins to blur the lines of decency and right from wrong. Too many of us fall into this pit of putting our identity in what others think and what is accepted. If the general consensus agrees sex sells, then why not start to project a woman's value to be sexual? Our identity starts to become a matter of public and/or business definition.

Our minds can get confused with the whirlwind of perceptions we have of ourselves, especially depending on the settings in which we find ourselves. My insecurities would dictate how I acted in public, which, and let's be honest, was not superb. The choices we make will either dictate consequences or will result in blessings. The choices I made were feeble and resulted in my sense of self-value degrading every day. Thoughts of being a better person would take over and bring me into a deep depression. I so desperately wanted to be the person my parents would be proud of, and better yet, someone of which I could be proud. Yet I didn't know how to change. I thought of myself as a weak individual who tried too hard to gain people's love.

Doubt would creep into my soul as to whether or not anyone loved me or could love me the way that I desired. My self-perception dictated the choices that caused me to negatively overcompensate for my shortcomings. My perception was I had no value and I would end up alone.

Loneliness is a powerful fear that drives us to put so much of our identity into what others think of us. We are wired to have that relational component to love and be loved. We were made in God's image. Think about that for a moment. To be made in God's image means God created us to be like Him. If God wired us to crave relationships then that means God craves relationships. He craves relationships with us. So if we are able to redirect our focus on fulfilling our loneliness with a relationship with God then it shouldn't matter what others think of us. We can finally realize we are not alone, and we were never alone. It took me a long time to figure that one out.

It turned out God was with me the whole time and my value was in Him. Hoewever, realizing something and growing into understanding it and internalizing it takes time. So in that beginning process, my identity switched from needing a man and a family, to my career being my identity. So even when I fully surrendered my heart to the Lord, I built my value and identity in something other than the Lord. I had given up the need for a man, indeed I felt it was a sacrifice for God, but this lead me to mistakenly think God led and blessed me in my career as a reward for that sacrifice. Proud moments would envelope my identity and take over my entire being. I loved climbing up that corporate ladder, no matter what the cost was to me. My identity relied upon the title and status I thought I had the privilege of conquering with God's blessing.

Moving up in my career was always part of the plan. Work hard to get where you want to be. Make yourself proud and make your family and friends proud. Keep working. Those were my thoughts when I was offered a position as a Sr. Financial Analyst with a bank. Going from a small private company to a large public company was the next step for me. Soon after I started, I was promoted to an impressive Assistant Vice President of the mortgage division. In my mind I was important and I was going places; however, the working conditions slowly began to wear on me. Working eighty hours a week on top of trying to serve at church felt overwhelming. Working until midnight several days a week with no light at the end of the tunnel drained me. My heart changed on whether or not it was worth it to climb the corporate ladder only to make my identity even more impressive. My purpose in life was to work hard and create that high status within this world. My purpose should have been living a life dedicated to Christ so I may bring other people to know the love and truth of God. I still missed the spiritual boat. In reality, I still sought the love and approval I craved. I had only redirected it into another pursuit.

Stressful situations tend to bring attention to different perspectives that we never thought about before. My goals for so long were to reach the top of the food chain within the accounting industry. I never thought of anything else. God put on my heart the desire to change gears. A change from the stressful climbing of the corporate ladder to a regular job working eight hours a day so I could focus more on helping others in ministry. This would mean possibly taking a pay cut and demotion in title. I soon realized money also fueled my identity. I never thought it did until it made me sick to my stomach to think of giving up the money; the money I worked so hard to earn and my annual bonus. What a reality check. My thought process was to rationalize reasons to "hang in there" with my current job until bonuses were paid out in a few months and then I would find a new job. However, God wanted to strip away my thoughts of money too. He wanted to make sure my new realized identity and dependencies would be completely in Him and not my career or money. God called me to do one thing, but my love for money prevented me from obeying His will for me. My identity was now wrapped in the functional rewards of my career. What was I supposed to do? Who was I without my big shot job? Eventually, God laid it on my heart to take my career off of the pedestal on which I had placed it.

It was the hardest thing I ever decided to do, but I eventually ended up quitting my job and giving up my potential bonus and all without a new job in sight. This was completely new for me. God wanted to clearly change and mold my perspective of who I thought I was and realign it with Him, but it had to be my choice. God had tried to get it through my thick head my worth was unrelated to my function or performance. It was linked to Him. God wants us to choose to have a relationship with Him. He wants us to choose to believe in Him enough to obey Him. After long bouts of prayer and a lot of anxiety, I decided to obey God in everything He wanted for me. I jumped into the unknown and I was terrified. It is one thing to say you have faith and another thing to act upon that faith.

So I made the jump and decided to quit my job. I was terrified to go down that path. I was truly going on faith, as I didn't have any idea when I would have a job or if I would be able to pay my bills when the money ran out. I had enough savings built up to last me about three months, but I knew if God wanted me to be obedient, He would provide for me. I ended up taking six weeks off to decompress and refocus my life on Christ. As it turned out, God blessed me with the time I needed and ultimately provided a job that exceeded my expectations. It was the best six weeks of my life. Upon realizing I had become free, I truly felt like an eagle soaring through the sky with its wings spread out and feeling the wind in its face. I was free from carrying the burden of putting status and money on a pedestal. My identity became my value in Christ and not something I did or earned. It turned from a functional identity into an intrinsic identity. My accomplishments or sense of acceptance finally had nothing to do with who I thought I was or could be. I finally understood I was a child of God and my performance in this world would not change my value in Christ. My understanding was finally grounded in my heart and not in my head. God provided me with a job that gave me the work/life balance I so desperately craved and still provided a management position I am proud and passionate about. What a truly amazing God we have.

The real message here is about letting go of past failures, past hurts, and old ways of thinking. The acknowledgment and admission to ourselves that we have failed in the past with controlling our actions helps us to move to that next cornerstone in our life. It opens our eyes on how to make the right decisions. In order for us to take those steps in the right direction we have to change our self-perception. Dwelling on feelings of not being worthy and viewing ourselves as failures will be reflected in our actions. How we perceive ourselves intertwines with the direction of our lives. We often get stuck in this pattern because our hearts and our minds are out of sync.

Intellectually, we have the knowledge our value is in Christ, but what does that mean? How does Christ view His followers? The key is in connecting the intellectual head knowledge with a heart transformation. It is the key to building up our belief and faith in Christ. Changing one's self-perception from negative to positive can be challenging and difficult, but it can be done. God speaks about this topic several times in the Bible.

He tells us that we are a masterpiece. He created us in a special and unique way so we can stand out in our own beautiful way from everyone else. We can fulfill His specific purpose uniquely designed for us as individuals. God does not make mistakes when creating us. We are who we are because God has a special plan for each and every one of us. You were not born a mistake or an accident because you are a child of His.

"For we are God's handiwork, created in Christ Jesus to do good works, which God prepared in advance for us to do." —Ephesians 2:10 (NIV)

We have a Heavenly Father who loves and adores us. His love is unconditional and we are His children. We may have earthly parents, but God is our ultimate sovereign Father and in the end, we will need to answer to Christ. Just as we want to please our parents and make them proud, we should also strive to seek and make God proud. We are special to Him. Amongst the billions of people in this world, God knows our name. He knows how many hairs we have on our head. He knows each and every one of our hurts and understands our struggles. He knows all of our victories and loves us each individually as if we were His only child.

"See what great love the Father has lavished on us, that we should be called children of God! And that is what we are! The reason the world does not know us is that it did not know him."
—1 John 3:1 (NIV)

When our value and identity is in Christ, we become conquerors. This was especially true for me and the life path that I chose for myself. I had to claw my way out of that muddy pit and conquer the demons that wanted to knock me down and keep me down. You might feel the same way. We go through so many struggles and see so much suffering in the world. It is easy to feel completely defeated and surrender to the desire to give up. It feels like you are climbing a steep mountain as you slowly stumble to the ground in exhaustion. It is critical in those times to remember, in Christ, we are conquerors. In Christ we have strength. With Christ in our lives, we can do anything because He will provide the strength we need. No problem is too big or small for God. With Him on our side we can overcome any obstacle that comes into our paths. We are conquering warriors in God's army.

"No, in all these things we are more than conquerors through him who loved us."
—Romans 8:37 (NIV)

As a child of God, we are free from condemnation. The destructive thoughts that go through our minds make us feel unworthy and undeserving to be a child of His and these need to be given to God. Through Christ we are a new being, a new creature. No longer do we need to condemn ourselves because Jesus Christ will never condemn us. We can lay our guilt and shame at Jesus' feet because we have been forgiven. The blessing of knowing Christ becomes the freedom we can feel from the heavy load of condemnation we once carried on our shoulders. It is a process to change our perspective, but knowing how God views His children and understanding our identity is in Christ gives us the freedom to be able to put into action positive thoughts ultimately overcoming negative thoughts.

"Therefore, there is now no condemnation for those who are in Christ Jesus." —Romans 8:1

We are chosen by the grace of God to be a part of His kingdom. God wants everyone to join His kingdom, no matter what our past may be. If your past is anything like mine, His grace forgives us and changes our heart's desire to be for Him instead of the darkness of this world. Grace is the unconditional forgiveness that is given to us even when we don't deserve it. God tells us our past does not matter; it is what we do now and in our future that matters. If we accept Christ into our lives as Lord and Savior, we are sealed by His power and given grace to be able to be connected with God. We are chosen to be His child. God is our acceptance and love. As I have thought about my past desires of wanting to be loved and accepted, the realization has come to me that God has always accepted me. It was I who did not accept Him. I did the one thing to God I feared people would do to me: rejection. This was one of those "a-ha" moments that come to us and are the switches that shine the light on our darkness.

> Praise be to the God and Father of our Lord Jesus Christ, who has blessed us in the heavenly realms with every spiritual blessing in Christ. For he chose us in him before the creation of the world to be holy and blameless in his sight. In love he predestined us for adoption to sonship through Jesus Christ, in accordance with his pleasure and will- to the praise of his glorious grace, which he has freely given to us in the One he loves. In him we have redemption through his blood, the forgiveness of sins, in accordance with the riches of God's grace that he lavished on us.
> —Ephesians 1:3-8

We can be strengthened by the power of God. In our weakness, we are strong. With God by our side, we can get through anything. As I went through my struggles of changing from my old self to my new self in Christ, I needed God every step of the way. He holds our hand throughout the day as a reminder

He is with us. We have to remember to lean on Him. God's character is amazing to me as I go through these verses, reminding me of the blessings of following Him. He cares about us. To have the knowledge of knowing we are unconditionally loved and we can do anything through Christ strengthens us and provides comfort and contentment in the midst of this crazy world. We are powerful and we are strong with Christ by our side.

"For who is God besides the Lord? And who is the Rock except our God? It is God who arms me with strength and keeps my way secure."
—Psalm 18:31-32

The realization of who we are in Christ and realizing the full potential of our value changes our perception and allows us to direct our lives to fulfill God's purpose and not our own. God is calling for us to live a bold, fearless life in pursuit of living out His will for us and giving Him all the glory.

Chapter 11

A Servant's Heart

When he had finished washing their feet, he put on his clothes and returned to his place. "Do you understand what I have done for you?" he asked them. "You call me 'Teacher' and 'Lord' and rightly so, for that is what I am. Now that I, your Lord and Teacher, have washed your feet, you also should wash one another's feet. I have set you an example that you should do as I have done for you. Very truly I tell you, no servant is greater than his master, nor is a messenger greater than the one who sent him. Now that you know these things, you will be blessed if you do them. — John 13:12-17 (NIV)

Having a servant's heart comes with a heart transformation and a desire to live for Christ. Fully surrendering to Christ meant giving up my past transgressions to God and asking for forgiveness. God created us in His image and that is where our true value and identity lie. As a Christian matures in their faith, the more they strive to become Christ-like in everything they do. One of the main components to being more Christ-like is having a servant's heart. As Jesus washed the feet of His disciples, so are we to wash the feet of others in service to them.

Part of having freedom in Christ is choosing to serve at a church and serve others. The focus needs to be taken off of our self-centered wants and desires and reflected onto helping people. It is healing to see smiles on other peoples' faces as you greet them at the door on a Sunday morning or know you helped make the coffee that is going to help keep people awake during the sermon. It is rewarding to know no matter what capacity in which we serve, we still have something to offer. It is important to realize it doesn't matter what we have done in the past, God is a majestic and sovereign God, and He will still use us to help others for His good and faithful will.

We often let our own thoughts of worthlessness get in the way of thinking we actually have something to offer. Well, we no longer need to listen to those lies. That is how Satan tries to knock us down from having full freedom in Christ. There are so many people out there who need a helping hand, words of encouragement, or a warm smile to let them know it's going to be okay. We need to start believing in God and trusting He can use us to serve others not because we are called to serve, but because of our *past transgressions*. People recovering from habitual sin have a unique perspective on life. We have seen more than we want to admit, and have gone through hell and back, mostly by our own accord. Because of that, we have the special ability to be able to have that compassion and empathy toward others who are struggling. We used to be the people others may have thought were hard to help or approach because we were a little "rough" around the edges. Who better to reach out to the lost souls that need guidance to see the light of truth than us?

Everyone has something to offer and can learn to have a servant's heart, but the heart must be in the right place. It may take a while to understand the dynamics of serving. I found my way through trial and error. The first time I tried getting back into the good grace of God by serving; I failed miserably. What I once thought was me doing good deeds and serving really became serving my own needs for the attention I received through that serving.

When I first went back to church years ago, I believed it was the right thing to do. The knowledge was in my head to go back and find God, so I put one foot in front of the other and decided to fall in line. The problem, as I had stated earlier, was my head and my heart did not connect. I was there because I knew that is what I was supposed to do, but I missed the relational component of what it meant to go to church. Serving was what everyone else did at church, so that was what I believed I needed to do. Since I was good with children, I signed up to be part of the kids program. I enjoyed being part of the program as I was able to act on stage in skits and help lead the kids in worship and song. I loved every minute of it—only I loved it a little too much. The realization came years later when I came to terms that my motivation was all about me and how I felt people perceived me. If everyone saw how much time and effort I put into volunteering, then it was a good thing for me. Everything I did while serving had a personal benefit in feeding my attention and acceptance complex. If it didn't benefit me, I wouldn't do it. Even as I look back now I can see I did not bear any fruit or blessings from God. Smiles were definitely being put on the children and they learned about God, but for myself, I was still dead inside. If we are serving to glorify God rather than ourselves then we should be able to see the fruit that grows from our efforts. I had no sense of what it meant to live for Christ. I felt like I had to take part in serving because it is what any Christian would do.

The bottom line was my heart transformation had not yet occurred, and in order to serve as Christ did, our hearts have to be full of grace, love, humility, and sacrifice. At the time, I served so I could say I was serving and it would be put on my resume of things I had done and accomplished. In hindsight, my main motivation in serving was to benefit me and secondarily because I thought the church needed the help. I believed they couldn't afford the staff it takes to effectively run a church, so that's why volunteers stepped in. That is all true, but I perceived serving as something the church as a business organization needed, and not something Jesus commanded us to do. I missed the mark on what serving was all about.

"Serve wholeheartedly as if you were serving the Lord, not people." —Ephesians 6:7 (NIV)

The key to anything and everything in life is Christ. Every problem this world has can be answered with the words of God. Every situation is intertwined with the next and woven in and out of trials and tribulations, even moments of happiness and joy. All of these connections are allowed and masterminded by the one and only Almighty Creator. It still blows my mind that we are His orchestra and He is the Conductor. If we do not follow His lead, the music begins to scramble and becomes noise instead of a beautiful elegant sound. Until I knew what a relationship with Christ looked like, I wouldn't recognize or understand the true meaning of serving.

Here is an honesty check: if you are serving at a church or any type of organization—what is your motive? Are you serving because it is what Jesus called you to do, or because it somehow benefits you either through recognition or a resume booster? Or are you not serving at all because you don't think you are good at anything or worthy of being able to serve?

These are questions I often ask myself. Our hearts naturally drift toward seeking the joy in serving due to a level of acceptance and recognition. At a certain level, it is okay to accept that recognition if you are serving with the right motivation. Perform a heart check to make sure the real reason you serve is for the love of Jesus Christ. If you are not serving, pray about where you can start and realize it will glorify God while helping you find a life of freedom in Christ.

"For you were called to freedom, brothers. Only do not use your freedom as an opportunity for the flesh, but through love serve one another."
—Galatians 5:13 (NIV)

It took me awhile to understand the true meaning of serving. It was to serve our Lord in whatever capacity He needs – not what I need. If my heart is focused on following Him, then the desire to serve would naturally be there. Five years ago, when I truly and fully surrendered my heart to Christ, my desire to serve without personal benefit caught on fire. However, my natural instinct, perhaps to make up for lost time, was a desire to serve in some big way. I thought, give me a huge project to do for you Lord, whatever it is, and I will do it. My heart was definitely in the right place, but I had to realize God has to see He can trust us with the little things first before He can trust us with the big things. The desire was overwhelming to dive right in, but the Lord kept me at His pace and on His timeline. I started out small, helping at the visitor table where I would answer questions for people who wanted to know more about the church and its activities. I also started to consistently attend a Bible study. As I realized later, His plan was to get me foundationally connected and to start growing in my faith through service to Him.

Eventually, as He started to see me consistently choosing to live a life that strived to glorify Him, He gave me that big project. I knew it had to come from God because it was something beyond what I ever thought I was capable of doing. It is not unusual for God to communicate in this way so we know without a shadow of a doubt that His hand is in it. God called me to start up and lead a women's recovery program at our church. I had no clue as to how to do it, but knew as long as I showed up and leaned on His strength, He would use me as His messenger to other women. This was a far stretch from what I used to think. I believed only people who strive to be perfect Christians in everything they do have the high honor of leading a Bible study. I soon found out we are all human and we all make mistakes. It is in our weakness that God uses us to our fullest capability. It is only when we know we are broken and humbled that God can use us as His messenger to help others.

Helping other women has become my heart's passion. It was not until I was fully healed and free that God used my past brokenness to help others.

I never imagined God would want me to serve in this capacity and in such an important role. I simply did not feel worthy. There were days and there are still days when I ask God, "Why me?" After all, I am no one in the grand scheme of things. Then I hear Him tell me in my heart with a loving and stern voice, *"Because my dear child you have a servant's heart who has surrendered to me. I have given you the strength to fulfill my purposes. You just need to choose to accept that I have chosen you for this role."* My heart skips a beat every time I think about God choosing me for this assignment. Because He chose me, I will trust in Him for strength to make the sacrifices to serve with love and compassion in this ministry to help women become free from habitual sin. There are moments of exhaustion. There are moments of heartbreak when someone doesn't understand the blessings that come with a life of surrendering to Christ. There are also moments of blessings in seeing women enter into the freedom of life in Christ.

There is always hope for a better life than the one we choose for ourselves. We have to learn to let go of our past. We need to learn our value is in Christ and not of this world or what our friends or family thinks of us, or even what we think of ourselves. We need to choose to lean on God as our Lord and Savior. We need to accept the life Christ has chosen for us and latch on to living a life with a servant's heart.

One thing I learned in serving is no job is too small or too big. Human nature will point out different tasks we think may be beneath us, or tasks that may appear to be overwhelming in work and we balk at the thought of putting in that many hours. I can tell you from experience God has chosen each task for each person and it is special and unique to that person and we should answer His call every time without fear and without hesitation.

I once had a friend who was down on herself because she only helped out with the laundry at church. She cleaned the towels and the tablecloths every other week, and she felt like it wasn't important or significant. She needed to stop thinking like that because every job has a purpose, and every job leads to helping others. If the tablecloths were not washed every week, then they would not be ready for the women's Bible study where an inviting table helps bring in women to a warm and accepting group of ladies. These tablecloths help set an environment where women accept Christ almost every week and it all started with washing the tablecloths that help set the tone for a friendly environment.

It reminds me of something someone once said about a mosquito. A mosquito can appear small and insignificant. All they do is fly around with no seeming purpose. They could be said to be behind the scenes. They are almost invisible until they decide to buzz in and around your ear. You start to notice the mosquito and try to swat it away as it grates on your nerves. Yet the mosquito keeps at it. So you have to ask yourself, if the mosquito is so small and insignificant, how could it make so much noise and impact on you? Just because the task we may do is considered a small task does not mean it doesn't make a lot of noise in the end. We may not always see the fruits of our labor, but it's the trust we have in God, knowing He will water the seed as long as we plant it.

Not all of us know what area God is calling us to serve in. Just praying for direction can be quite frustrating as often silence is all we experience. Don't give up; that silence may be God's way of trying to tell you that you need to do something in parallel with praying. Start trying different areas in your church to serve and see if you feel anything toward that area of service. Start off small and work your way into different areas. There is something to be said at filling a small need for a church. God gives each of us special spiritual gifts we can use together as a church body to do good works for God's purposes. It is important we know what each of our gifts are so we can help utilize the gifts God has granted us.

We have different gifts, according to the grace given to each of us. If your gift is prophesying, then prophesy in accordance with your faith; if it is serving, then serve; if it is teaching, then teach; if it is to encourage, then give encouragement; if it is giving, then give generously; if it is to lead, do it diligently; if it is to show mercy, do it cheerfully. —Romans 12:6-8

A little caveat is in store here. It is important to understand not all of us will be good at the same thing. Some of us are not called to lead Bible studies, and that's okay. Some of us are not called to serve with children, and that's okay. Some of us are not called to be greeters, and that's okay. That's why each and every one of us has a special place in the church. Together we make the full church body. So know your gifts God has given you and pray about where God wants you to serve. If you do not know what your spiritual gifts are, you can go to www.spiritualgifttest.com and take the test to find out.

> Just as a body, though one, has many parts, but all its many parts form one body, so it is with Christ. For we were all baptized by one Spirit so as to form one body—whether Jews or Gentiles, slave or free—and we were all given the one Spirit to drink. Even so the body is not made up of one part but of many.
> Now if the foot should say, "Because I am not a hand, I do not belong to the body," it would not for that reason stop being part of the body. And if the ear should say, "Because I am not an eye, I do not belong to the body," it would not for that reason stop being part of the body. If the whole body were an eye, where would the sense of hearing be? If the whole body were an ear, where would the sense of smell be? But in fact God has placed the parts in the

body, every one of them, just as he wanted them to be. If they were all one part, where would the body be? As it is, there are many parts, but one body.

The eye cannot say to the hand, "I don't need you!" And the head cannot say to the feet, "I don't need you!" On the contrary, those parts of the body that seem to be weaker are indispensable, and the parts that we think are less honorable we treat with special honor. And the parts that are unpresentable are treated with special modesty, while our presentable parts need no special treatment. But God has put the body together, giving greater honor to the parts that lacked it, so that there should be no division in the body, but that its parts should have equal concern for each other. If one part suffers, every part suffers with it; if one part is honored, every part rejoices with it. Now you are the body of Christ, and each one of you is a part of it. And God has placed in the church first of all apostles, second prophets, third teachers, then miracles, then gifts of healing, of helping, of guidance, and of different kinds of tongues. Are all apostles? Are all prophets? Are all teachers? Do all work miracles? Do all have gifts of healing? Do all speak in tongues? Do all interpret? Now eagerly desire the greater gifts. —1 Corinthians 12:12-30

Developing a servant's heart has an impact on transforming the heart and leads to healing. Being able to help others, even in something small, helps give the importance and the worth so desperately needed after a past of habitual sin. Serving others builds relationships with others and gives that connection and accountability lost so long ago when we separated ourselves from Christ in our sinful behavior. It takes the focus off of us and puts Jesus Christ at the forefront of our minds. We are called to love our neighbors and our enemies. We are called to wash people's feet in service as Jesus washed the disciples' feet. Jesus came to us as a servant. His whole purpose on this earth was to be of service to us. He served us in the biggest way possible. He gave His life on the cross to pay the debt of our sins so we may have a relationship with God. He has the ultimate servant's heart and I don't know about you, but I want to live and glorify Christ as He sacrificially lived for me. It is time for us to become fearless in our new identities in Christ to fulfill the purpose of bringing people into God's eternal kingdom.

Chapter 12

Fearless

———— ✳ ————

"We all want progress, but if you're on the wrong road, progress means doing an about turn and walking back to the right road; in that case, the man who turns back soonest is the most progressive."
— C.S. Lewis

I have been on many wrong roads in my lifetime and I am sure I will probably drift onto many more wrong roads before my time is up here on this earth. Living a God-fearing life, and living it fearlessly in this world is a hard task, especially in this world full of darkness. It is vitally important the light of Christ is brought back into this world so people can know what it is like living a life to glorify Christ. How is that done? Start by being fearless in praying, being obedient, in hope and faith, in surrender, and in love. In other words, fearless in taking action to live a Christ-filled life no matter what others think of us. That is the hard part. Too many of us put too much value into what others think and we adapt our identity into what others want and not what we are meant to be in God's image. We need to pray for courage, so when we do start to feel fear or embarrassment, we have the strength to overcome those emotions. Are you tired of living a life that feels like it has no purpose, a life in which you feel like you are spinning your wheels and getting nowhere?

Fearless Surrender

If you are a control freak like me, this is one of the toughest things to do. Admitting my way is not always the best way goes against my nature. I tend to be impatient and when I want something, I want it now. Sometimes I try to rationalize taking things into my own hands by telling myself Jesus must be too busy right now to give me what I want. That's right, I'm going to help Him out a little bit and take this off His plate. Countless times I ended up making a complete mess. God can move mountains and perform miracles, so what in the world makes me think He is too busy to handle my wants and desires? More often than not, God is telling me to wait because He is working on something so much better than I ever imagined or He is telling me no because He wants me to go down a different road that will bless my life even more.

I used to think by fully surrendering to Christ, it was more of a sacrifice on my part than His. I felt like I would have to give up so much of my life and have to follow all of these rules and give up the things I like doing. It required too much effort on my part. Then, what would my friends think if I became a "Jesus freak" or a "Bible thumper?" Would I lose those friendships? The answer, to my surprise, ended up being quite different. After a few years of fully surrendering to Him, I realized it is not a sacrifice, but a blessing. Keep in mind, fully surrendering is not as easy as it sounds. To get to that point, I had to learn to let go of my past. This was extremely difficult in that I had become obsessed with trying to fill that empty void inside; obsessed to the point of trying anything and everything to experience that love and fulfillment as I thought it was defined. It was not until I surrendered to Christ that the emptiness began to fill up with God's love. What I did not understand for so long is Christ had always accepted me, but I had put up this barrier of self-centered control that quenched God's efforts to reach me. Upon finally realizing this, I felt the truth of His love and felt accepted. I had asked for and understood forgiveness, let go of my past, and forgave myself. I fearlessly surrendered. If you have not surrendered it's time to do that. I promise your life will be like a wilted flower that has come back to a life full of blessings.

Luke 7 tells a story about a woman who had lived a sinful life and upon finding out that Jesus was having dinner at a Pharisee's (Simon's) house, she went to the house with a jar of perfume. As she stood behind Jesus she wept and began to wet His feet with her tears and to dry them with her hair. She kissed His feet and then poured the expensive perfume on them. Simon was stunned Jesus allowed this sinful woman to touch Him and expressed his dismay.

Jesus told Simon, "Two people owed money to a certain moneylender. One owed him five hundred denarii, and the other fifty. Neither of them had the money to pay him back, so he forgave the debts of both. Now which of them will love him more?"

Simon replied, "I suppose the one who had the bigger debt forgiven."

"You have judged correctly," Jesus said.

Then he turned toward the woman and said to Simon, "Do you see this woman? I came into your house. You did not give me any water for my feet, but she wet my feet with her tears and wiped them with her hair. You did not give me a kiss, but this woman, from the time I entered, has not stopped kissing my feet. You did not put oil on my head, but she has poured perfume on my feet. Therefore, I tell you, her many sins have been forgiven —as her great love has shown. But whoever has been forgiven little loves little."

Then Jesus said to her, "Your sins are forgiven."

As I read this story I reflected on my past sins and knew there were many to forgive. Satan wants us to feel like our sins are too great to be forgiven, but this story demonstrates the greater the life of sin that has been forgiven, the greater the impact on gratefulness and understanding of the depth of Christ's forgiveness. This, in turn, results in a greater desire to live to glorify Christ. If you have a past like mine, you can be confident and fearless in your pursuit of Christ because no sin is too dark to be forgiven. What a huge relief.

Fearless Hope and Faith

Hope and faith are linked together. Faith believes in a God who is unseen to our naked eye, but that lives within our soul and can be seen in the design of creation. A fearless faith in Christ means a willingness to take the necessary steps of obedience to pursue the life God has planned for us. That is the path to a life full of peace and joy. God did not want me to live a life where drugs and sex were my idol, but He sure knew how He could use it for good. You can be that person too. You can be that person who has enough hope and faith Christ will set you free from your habitual sins. You can be that person God uses to help others become free through setting an example of a God centered life. Hope is more than what we think of it in today's terms. We use the word so loosely, but when you intertwine hope with faith, it takes on a whole new meaning.

Hope is the confident expectation of joy. I know what some of you may be thinking. It is hard to have hope when there is no end in sight to your pain and struggles. It is hard to see hope when everything in your life is turned upside down. Trust me, the path to freedom is to strive to change your way of thinking. Hope doesn't mean a feeling of expectation and desire for a certain thing to happen. The word hope is often used incorrectly. From the Christian perspective, it means to look forward to a joy grounded in the gift of eternal life with God. So in order to have hope, you have to have faith; faith in a God who loves you unconditionally; faith in a God who knows you better than yourself and stands next to you in every situation. It is knowing you have eternal life by having faith in our Lord and Savior that is that hope. It is the hope to keep moving forward no matter what happens in this life because we are working toward eternal life where there will be no more tears, pain, and suffering. That is where my hope lies. It makes it easier to get through every trial and tribulation that comes my way, because no matter what happens, I know through my faith that I have hope and joy that is in being with Jesus Christ forever.

This is my heart's desire for everyone in this world. If you are a non-believer and you are willing to ask Jesus to show you He is real and can make good on His promises, He will. He is waiting for you to give up control and give it all to Him. When you do, He will show you unconditional love and the joy it provides. If you are a believer, stop and think about the negativity that you may be allowing in your life and realign it with the promises of God. Stop asking where God is and start seeking and acknowledging Him because He has always stood right next to you waiting for you to take His hand.

God is always with us, especially when going through difficult times. It is important to stop and contemplate what He is doing by allowing us to go through these different situations. What is He orchestrating? I can attest by experience God will always use a bad situation for good; we may not see it or understand it at the time, but it is the trust, faith, and hope we have in Christ that we know He is a good God. We grow in our relationship with Christ through our brokenness and trials. They are a necessary part of spiritual growth. If nothing but good happens to us, we get complacent and will miss the blessings God has for us as we go through different trials. In addition, we may also miss out on the opportunity to help someone else with our own experiences.

So what does it look like to stay anchored in hope?

It means we can forgive as Christ forgave us. We can have joy even through the tough times because we know the outcome is going to be eternal life.

"Consider it pure joy, my brothers and sisters, whenever you face trials of many kinds, because you know that the testing of your faith produces perseverance." –James 1:2-3 (NIV)

> We are hard pressed on every side, but not crushed; perplexed, but not in despair; persecuted, but not abandoned; struck down, but not destroyed. We always carry around in our body the death of Jesus, so that the life of Jesus may also be revealed in our body. For we who are alive are always being given over to death for Jesus' sake, so that his life may also be revealed in our mortal body. So then, death is at work in us, but life is at work in you.
>
> It is written: "I believed; therefore I have spoken." Since we have that same spirit of faith, we also believe and therefore speak, because we know that the one who raised the Lord Jesus from the dead will also raise us with Jesus and present us with you to himself. All this is for your benefit, so that the grace that is reaching more and more people may cause thanksgiving to overflow to the glory of God.
>
> Therefore we do not lose heart. Though outwardly we are wasting away, yet inwardly we are being renewed day by day. For our light and momentary troubles are achieving for us an eternal glory that far outweighs them all. So we fix our eyes not on what is seen, but on

what is unseen, since what is seen is temporary, but what is unseen is eternal.
—2 Corinthians 4:8-18 (NIV)

Fearless Obedience

To be obedient means to have enough belief in
Christ to follow Him without question. This requires
mounds of faith and trust God's plans and purpose
for us are perfect. A few years back I started what I
call my faith bucket. I started it because I realized
hindsight is 20/20 in understanding our past experiences and so every time I saw God working in my
life, I took the memory of His good works and what
He did for me and put it in my faith bucket. Then,
when I felt God calling me to do something that felt
too scary, I pulled out the faith bucket and reviewed
the mounds of memories. This process reminded
me of God's faithfulness and He will continue to be
faithful in the new calling.

God has called me to do a lot over these last
couple of years. Sometimes they were small things,
which felt easy enough to obey, and some things
were big. It was the big things that often felt completely beyond my abilities where I would find
myself lost in what to do. However, I have learned
when I felt this sense of feeling lost, it was an indi-
cator the leading was from God. The only way for
His will to be followed was for me to lean completely on Him and let Him do His thing through me.

One of those big things was to call me to minister to women who struggle with habitual sin. Another was when He called me to quit my job and give up my financial security and a bonus. Then He called me to lead a Bible study for women. These are all examples of His callings that, to be honest, scared the daylights out of me and ignited severe insecurities. Needless to say, the conversations I had with God on these issues were intense. It would go something like this: "I can't Lord; there is no way," and God would respond, through an understanding in my heart, this isn't something meant for me to do within my own strength. It is meant for me to do in His strength so it glorifies Him.

The process of Him calling me to something, then my resistance, and then ultimately surrendering to His leading and obedience to His will changed my life for the better. The blessings that God has given to me because of my obedience go beyond what I ever thought possible.

Following Christ is not going to church on Sunday and saying you believe. It requires us to act upon our faith to fulfill God's purpose for our lives, which is ultimately to share God's light with others and bring them to Christ. We are meant to be far greater than anything we could conjure up for ourselves in this lifetime. It is time to be fearless in our obedience and be willing to fearlessly jump in the name of Christ. Our lives are so much better when we follow what our almighty creator has planned for us instead of our own plans. Are you willing to jump with me in faith and obedience and see where God takes you?

Fearless Prayer

When we accept Christ as Lord and Savior, we are changed forever as a child of God. That is only the beginning of our growth and maturing in Him. A critical component to growing and maturing in Him is to be regularly on our knees praying. This is such a crucial step to changing from the old self to a new self in Christ. It is important to finally say enough is enough and realize we can't handle things on our own strength. When we are willing to admit we are inadequate, then we open up our hearts to let Christ in. Without prayer, your relationship with God will be stagnant. You might as well have no relationship.

Many people do not know how to pray and are intimidated by it. They feel like they have to have the right words in order to reach God. However, it is not like that; prayer is a simple conversation between you and Christ. There is no right or wrong way to pray. If you have no idea how to pray, simply start by saying, "Lord I need your help" and tell Him what's on your mind.

Prayer is one of the most important steps in strengthening our walk with Christ. Yet it is often taken for granted. Most people tend to pray as a last resort when they have a massive problem and only after they have exhausted all their own problem-solving ideas. Or they tend to pray for other people and not for themselves. Praying for these things is not wrong as God hears all of our prayers, but it is important to remember to pray fearlessly not only during the bad times, but during the good times. We need to live with a heart of gratitude and thankfulness. We also need to pray for ourselves. When I ask for prayer requests during Bible study, I always tell people to put down a request for someone else and then put down a request for themselves. Most people tend to think that other peoples' struggles are more important than their own little problems and so tend not to pray for themselves. I'll tell you a little secret. God wants us to spill our guts with what happens during each day. He wants to hear what problems we are facing and what blessings we have received. That is exactly what a relationship is all about. He wants to hear about our day.

We can only begin to touch the sky of heaven when our knees are hitting the ground. It isn't until we start to pray fearlessly and consistently that we begin to see changes in our behavior and our lives. It causes a ripple effect. Putting time aside to pray each day brings us closer to God and fills us with a sense of peace and joy in our daily walk with Him. Over time, others start to notice the subtle changes in us and they begin to want the same experience. It all starts with prayer. Everything and every day should start with prayer. One thing I learned to do over the last few years was not only spill my day and worries to God, but to also thank Him for everything He has done for me. I have learned to be specific in my prayers as well. The more specific we are in our prayers, the more we can see God working within our prayers and how He answers them. Another critical factor is to listen. Many people think prayer is a one-way dialogue with God, but in reality, it goes both ways. God definitely speaks to our hearts, but the problem for a lot of people is they do not know how to be quiet and listen during their prayer time. It is not difficult, but may take some practice. It is hard to be still and tune in to the voice of God in our hearts. Trust me, it is real and it works. Start trying to think of yourself as a prayer warrior with the goal of building a relationship with Christ. Oh, and one more thing, when I talk about being on your knees, it does not always mean figuratively. God listens to us at all times of the day and in all circumstances. He is a thought and a word away. All you have to do is acknowledge Him and speak like He is physically standing right next to you. It is that real.

Fearless Love

To love means to be vulnerable to opening up your heart and allowing people to be close. It is straight up terrifying if you ask me, but it was not always that way. In my journey, I went from wanting love so bad, I would do anything to get it—to getting my heart broken so many times I shut my heart down, put it in a box, and used super glue to seal it. I went from one extreme to the other. It wasn't until I fully surrendered to Christ that I slowly started to unseal that box and let my heart breathe a little bit. Jt was a slow process as I feared getting hurt and I did not want to go through the pain of getting my heart broken again. When I think about it, I could probably have lived my life with my heart sealed up forever, but what kind of life would it have been? God wants us to have quality of life. He calls us to love because He is love. He is every standard of love and every kind of love. His character is love. Since He built us in His image, He also created us to love and to be loved. We are wired to be relational. So if I continued to live a life with my heart sealed up in a super glued box then I would have lived a life deprived of the blessings of having a true relationship with Christ.

During those times when my heart was severely broken, I didn't have Christ in my life. Once I learned to love Christ and to accept His love, then love itself didn't feel so scary. I found myself opening up again and building friendships and my life began to fill up with blessing after blessing. We need to love each other in this world.

In order for us to truly learn to love and allow ourselves to be loved, we need to take off the many masks we often hide behind. I used to have them too. I would change my personality dependent upon who I was with and that meant that no one really knew the real me. If people don't know the real us then how can they love us for who we really are? This takes courage. Overcoming the fear of taking off the mask(s) and letting people know we are imperfect and may have baggage takes a lot of bravery, but love heals all. When we start to outwardly and unconditionally love others, we begin to see perhaps others can love us as we are too. That opens the door to allow us to love ourselves as who we are in Christ.

*****

I don't know where you are in life right now. Maybe you are in the midst of a painful struggle and realize you are using substances to cope with and ease the pain. Maybe you are searching for that quick fix to make you feel better and find yourself in a vicious cycle from which there feels to be no way out. Maybe you are enslaved to negative thoughts that constantly tear you down. Or maybe, as you read this, you realize you know someone who is going through something similar. My hope is you can take my story and know there is a light at the end of the tunnel.

No longer do we need to be slaves to our fear of being hopelessly inadequate and purposeless in life. It is not until we find the courage to be fearless in a pursuit of Christ and to seek Him will we start to live the life that God has planned for us. Rick Warren once said, "The greatest tragedy is not death itself, it is living a life without purpose."

There is no sin too great for Jesus to forgive. If Christ can forgive someone like me after my countless sins and all I have done to disgrace Him, then He can forgive you too. All you have to do is ask. Maybe you feel like you are in a pitch-black room and there is no light to find your way. I pray my story can be that flashlight in your dark room. My hope is for you to be inspired to action. Take control of your life and lay your burdens at God's feet. He is longing for a close relationship with you and He is longing to provide healing for you. He is waiting for you to surrender to Him. We are called to action in living a life that glorifies Christ. Let's take our brokenness and let God use it for good. Let God rescue you as He has rescued me.

Epilogue

―――――― ✳ ――――――

When God called me to write this book I immediately told Him there is no way. I am an accountant. I work with numbers all day primarily because I did not do well with English in school. It was a constant battle for me to write papers and express myself through words. This was completely beyond me. God and I went back and forth for about six months until He gave me confirmation after confirmation that He actually called me to put my story down on paper. I had no other choice but to follow His lead and be obedient in His calling for me. With fear in my soul I started to write.

Writing my story required me to be vulnerable and transparent to a point that pushed my boundaries and exceeded my comfort levels, yet I continued to write. This was a definite learning experience for me and I know I have grown in my faith throughout this process. There were times that I typed on my keyboard as water welled up in my eyes and tears poured down my cheeks as I pushed myself to go back to a dark time. Even though there were moments of sadness there, were also moments of feeling completely overwhelmed with God's love and the peacefulness that comes with understanding of what Christ did for me. He pulled me out of my muddy pit not once, but several times and still said, "I love you." His unconditional love pulled me through and pushed me toward true freedom. God's grace is what got me to where I am today and only by His love am I the person He has called me to be.

My hope is my story will give you the inspiration to take action—whatever that may be to you. It may be deciding you want a relationship with Christ. Or it may be you want to re-commit your life to Christ and get back on track. Whatever you feel that call to action may be for you, my hope is you know there is hope for a better life than what you could have ever imagined with our Lord and Savior Jesus Christ. In your weakness and your brokenness may you allow Jesus to use you in His purpose. Let's shine God's light on an imperfect and dark world because in the end, it is not this world that we live for, but eternal life with Jesus Christ.

If you have never prayed the prayer to accept Jesus in your life and you would like to, it is easy. Below is a prayer of salvation you can pray. If you decide to pray this prayer, may I say congratulations on making the first step to a brand new life and a brand new you. I will be praying for you and I am so excited for you.

If you are in the position of already accepting Christ earlier in your life, but have lost your way, I pray you decide to recommit your life to Christ, for He is the only way, the truth, and the life. Below is a prayer of recommitment that may help you get right with God.

Prayer of Salvation

Dear Heavenly Father, I know I am sinner, Lord, and I understand you sent your only Son to die on the cross for my sins. Please forgive me for not living a life glorifying you. I want to spend the rest of my life in your kingdom, Lord, and I know it requires repentance and me turning from my sin. I know, with your help and your strength, I can leave my old life behind me. I want to transform my old self into a new self that lives a life for your purpose, Lord, and not my own. I ask you fill me with the power of the Holy Spirit so I may be a child of yours. Amen.

Prayer of Recommitment

Lord, I have strayed far from the path of righteousness and I ask that you forgive me. I know now that taking control of my life has not done me any good and it is far from what you want for me. I know you love me Lord and I want to recommit myself to living a life that glorifies you. I pray you give me the strength and wisdom to turn from my sins and rebuild my relationship with you. The last thing I want is to be separated from you and my past choices have done that. Please transform my heart into desiring to be close to you, Lord, as I want to be right with you, Lord. Amen.

We are all continuous works in progress and will be until our work is done here on this earth. We will continue to go through trials and tribulations throughout our life, but when we have God on our side, we can get through those struggles a little bit easier and still with the peace and comfort of knowing where our home is going to be eternally. I pray you live a life that shines God's light and realize our purpose here on earth is to help bring others to Christ and to show His love through our actions. Let's live a bold life on faith and put our faith into action because being rescued inspires rescuing. We can now be the rescuers.

Light at the End of the Tunnel
By Courtney Smith

Falling full of darkness
Wish I were unconscious

Full of mixed emotions
Complete at my lowness

Trying to dig deep for joy but all I do is destroy

Looking for love in all the wrong places
I can't remember all their faces

All I want to do is cope
And I keep thinking there is no hope

Right when I am about to quit
Jesus dug me out of my pit

A light at the end of the tunnel shown bright
Even thought it was the dead of night

He gave me hope to continue on
Little by little I turned into a swan

Darkness turned into a bright shiny light
And now I am standing upright

A light at the end of the tunnel shown bright
Because Jesus filled me with pure delight

women 18⟲

changing lives 180 degrees

If you would like additional encouragement
come follow me at:

Women180.org

Where we can start to change lives
180 degrees.

Feel free to contact me at
Courtney.Smith@women180.org
I appreciate the feedback and would love to
encourage you and pray for you.

 @women180_cs    /women180

CPSIA information can be obtained at www.ICGtesting.com
Printed in the USA
BVOW08s1340090316

439653BV00002B/87/P